Harvard Business Review

ON

RETAILING AND MERCHANDISING

THE HARVARD BUSINESS REVIEW PAPERBACK SERIES

The series is designed to bring today's managers and professionals the fundamental information they need to stay competitive in a fast-moving world. From the preeminent thinkers whose work has defined an entire field to the rising stars who will redefine the way we think about business, here are the leading minds and landmark ideas that have established the *Harvard Business Review* as required reading for ambitious businesspeople in organizations around the globe.

Other books in the series:

Harvard Business Review Interviews with CEOs

Harvard Business Review on Advances in Strategy

Harvard Business Review on Appraising Employee Performance

Harvard Business Review on Becoming a High Performance Manager

Harvard Business Review on Brand Management

Harvard Business Review on Breakthrough Leadership

Harvard Business Review on Breakthrough Thinking

Harvard Business Review on Bringing Your Whole Self to Work

Harvard Business Review on Building Personal and Organizational Resilience

Harvard Business Review on the Business Value of IT

Harvard Business Review on Change

Harvard Business Review on Compensation

Harvard Business Review on Corporate Ethics

Harvard Business Review on Corporate Governance

Harvard Business Review on Corporate Responsibility

Harvard Business Review on Corporate Strategy

Harvard Business Review on Crisis Management

Harvard Business Review on Culture and Change

Harvard Business Review on Customer Relationship Management

Other books in the series (continued):

Harvard Business Review on the Mind of the Leader

Harvard Business Review on Motivating People

Harvard Business Review on Negotiation and Conflict Resolution

Harvard Business Review on Nonprofits

Harvard Business Review on Organizational Learning

Harvard Business Review on the Persuasive Leader

Harvard Business Review on Pricing

Harvard Business Review on Profiting from Green Business

Harvard Business Review on Strategic Alliances

Harvard Business Review on Strategic Renewal

Harvard Business Review on Strategic Sales Management

Harvard Business Review on Strategies for Growth

Harvard Business Review on Supply-Chain Management

Harvard Business Review on Talent Management

Harvard Business Review on Teams That Succeed

Harvard Business Review on the Tests of a Leader

Harvard Business Review on Top-Line Growth

Harvard Business Review on Turnarounds

Harvard Business Review on Women in Business

Harvard Business Review on Work and Life Balance

Harvard Business Review

ON

RETAILING AND
MERCHANDISING

A HARVARD BUSINESS REVIEW PAPERBACK

The *Harvard Business Review* articles in this collection are available as
individual reprints. Discounts apply to quantity purchases. For information and ordering, please contact Customer Service, Harvard Business
School Publishing, Boston, MA 02163. Telephone: (617) 783-7500 or
(800) 988-0886, 8 A.M. to 6 P.M. Eastern Time, Monday through Friday.
Fax: (617) 783-7555, 24 hours a day. E-mail: custserv@hbsp.harvard.edu.

Library of Congress cataloging information forthcoming
ISBN 978-1-4221-4592-0

Contents

Harvard Business Review

ON

RETAILING AND
MERCHANDISING

The Old Pillars of New Retailing

LEONARD L. BERRY

Executive Summary

DESPITE THE HARSH REALITIES of retailing, the illusion persists that magical tools can help companies overcome the problems of fickle consumers, price-slashing competitors, and mood swings in the economy. Such wishful thinking holds that retailers will thrive if only they communicate better with customers through e-mail, employ hidden cameras to learn how customers make purchase decisions, and analyze scanner data to tailor special offers and manage inventory. But the truth is, there are no quick fixes.

In the course of his extensive research on dozens of retailers, Leonard Berry found that the best companies create value for their customers in five interlocking ways. Whether you're running a physical store, a catalog business, an e-commerce site, or a combination of the three, you have to offer your customers superior solutions to

1

their needs, treat them with respect, and connect with them on an emotional level. You also have to set prices fairly and make it easy for people to find what they need, pay for it quickly, and then move on. None of these pillars is new, and each sounds exceedingly simple, but don't be fooled—implementing these axioms in the real world is surprisingly difficult.

The author illustrates how some retailers have built successful operations by attending to these common-sense ways of dealing with their customers and how others have failed to do so.

Everyone who glances at a newspaper knows that the retailing world is brutally competitive. The demise of Montgomery Ward in the realm of bricks and mortar as well as the struggles of eToys on-line—to choose only two recent examples—make it clear that no retailer can afford to be complacent because of previous successes or rosy predictions about the future of commerce.

Despite the harsh realities of retailing, the illusion persists that magical tools, like Harry Potter's wand, can help companies overcome the problems of fickle consumers, price-slashing competitors, and mood swings in the economy. The wishful thinking holds that retailers will thrive if only they communicate better with customers through e-mail, employ hidden cameras to learn how customers make purchase decisions, and analyze scanner data to tailor special offers and manage inventory.

But the truth of the matter is, there are no quick fixes. Yes, technology can help any business operate more effectively, but many new advances are still poorly understood—and in any case, retailing can't be reduced to tools and techniques. Over the past eight years, I've analyzed dozens of retail companies to understand the underlying differences between outstanding and mediocre performers. My research includes interviews with senior and middle managers and frontline employees, observations of store operations, and extensive reviews of published and internal company materials. I've found that the best retailers create value for their customers in five interlocking ways. Doing a good job in just three or four of the ways won't cut it; competitors will rush to exploit weakness in any of the five areas. If one of the pillars of a successful retailing operation is missing, the whole edifice is weakened.

The key is focusing on the total customer experience. Whether you're running physical stores, a catalog business, an e-commerce site, or a combination of the three, you have to offer customers superior solutions to their needs, treat them with real respect, and connect with them on an emotional level. You also have to set prices fairly and make it easy for people to find what they need, pay for it, and move on. These pillars sound simple on paper, but they are difficult to implement in the real world. Taking each one in turn, we'll see how some retailers have built successful operations by attending to these commonsense ways of dealing with customers, and how others have failed to pay them the attention they require.

Pillar 1: Solve Your Customers' Problems

It has become commonplace for companies to talk about selling solutions rather than products or services. But what does this really mean for retailers? Put simply, it

means that customers usually shop for a reason: they
have a problem—a need—and the retailer hopes to provide the solution. It's not enough, for example, just to sell
high-quality apparel—many retailers do that. Focusing
on solutions means employing salespeople who know
how to help customers find clothing that fits and flatters,
having tailors on staff and at the ready, offering home
delivery, and happily placing special orders. Every
retailer hopes to meet its customers' pressing needs;
some do it much better than others.

The Container Store provides its customers with
superior solutions. The 22-store chain, based in Dallas,
averages double-digit annual sales growth by selling
something that absolutely everyone needs: storage and
organization products. From boxes and trunks to
hangers, trays, and shelving systems, each store carries
up to 12,000 different products.

The Container Store's core strategy is the same today
as it was in 1978, when the company was founded: to
improve customers' lives by giving them more time and
space. The company accomplishes this mission well. It
starts with the selection of merchandise, which must
meet criteria for visibility, accessibility, and versatility.
The company's philosophy is that its products should
allow people to see what they've stored and get at it easily. The merchandise must also be versatile enough to
accommodate customers' particular requirements.

Store organization is another key ingredient of superior solutions at the Container Store. The merchandise is
organized in sections such as kitchen, closet, laundry,
office, and so on. Many products are displayed in several
sections because they can solve a variety of problems. A
sweater box, for example, can also store office supplies.
Plastic trash cans can also be used for dog food and recy-
clables. Individual products are often combined and sold

as a system—thus, parents in the store who want to equip their children for summer camp may find a trunk filled with a laundry bag, a toothbrush case, a first-aid pouch, leakproof bottles, a "critter catcher," and other items.

Great service is another component of the Container Store's ability to solve its customers' storage problems. The company is very careful about hiring; it patiently waits until it finds just the right person for a position. Container Store employees are well trained to demonstrate how products work and to propose solutions to complex home organizational problems. They are also treated very well, both in terms of pay and in less tangible ways. In fact, the Container Store was ranked the best place to work in the country in 1999 and 2000 by *Fortune* magazine.

A relentless focus on solutions may sound simple, but it's not. The Container Store has many imitators, but none have matched it. Many businesses have only the fuzziest concept of selling solutions. Department store chains, for example, have stumbled in recent years. They lost their one-stop shopping advantage by eliminating many merchandise categories outside of apparel and housewares. And even as they focused on apparel, they lost ground both to specialty retailers that have larger category selections and to discounters that have lower prices. Finally, they lost their customer service advantage by employing salespeople who often are little more than poorly trained order takers. As a result, these stores do a relatively poor job of solving customers' problems. That's probably why only 72% of consumers shopped in department stores in 2000 compared with 85% in 1996.

Clearly, the lesson here is that you must understand what people need and how you're going to fill that need better than your competitors. The Container Store has figured this out; many department stores and other struggling retailers must go back to the beginning and answer these basic questions.

Pillar 2: Treat Customers with R-e-s-p-e-c-t

The best retailers show their customers what Aretha Franklin sang about: respect. Again, this is absolutely basic, and most retail executives would say that of course they treat customers with respect. But it just isn't so.

Everyone has stories to tell about disrespectful retailing. You're in an electronics store, looking for assistance to buy a DVD player or a laptop computer. You spot a couple of employees by their uniforms and badges, but they're deep in conversation. They glance in your direction but continue to ignore you. After awhile, you walk out, never to return.

Or you're in a discount store, looking for planters that have been advertised at a low price. You go to the store's garden center but cannot find the planters. This time, you succeed in flagging down an employee. You ask about the planters, but she just mumbles "I dunno" and walks away. Frustrated, you go to the customer service desk and ask the clerk where you might find the advertised planters. He suggests that you try the garden center. Once again, you head for the exit.

It's easy to go on. Stories about women trying to buy cars, as everyone knows, are enough to make your hair curl. The fact is, disrespectful retailing is pervasive. In the 2000 Yankelovich Monitor study of 2,500 consumers, 68% of those surveyed agreed with the statement that "Most of the time, the service people that I deal with for the products and services that I buy don't care much about me or my needs."

Disrespectful retailing isn't just about bored, rude, and unmotivated service workers. Cluttered, poorly organized stores, lack of signage, and confusing prices all show lack of respect for customers.

The best retailers translate the basic concept of respect into a set of practices built around people, policies, and place:

- They select, prepare, and manage their people to exhibit competence, courtesy, and energy when dealing with customers.

- They institute policies that emphasize fair treatment of customers—regardless of their age, gender, race, appearance, or size of purchase or account. Likewise, their prices, returns policy, and advertising are transparent.

- They create a physical space, both inside and outside the store, that is carefully designed to value customers' time.

In 1971, a 30-year-old entrepreneur named Len Riggio bought a floundering Manhattan bookshop called Barnes & Noble. Today, Barnes & Noble is the nation's largest bookseller, with fiscal 1999 sales of $3.3 billion. Respect for the customer has been at the heart of the company's rise.

Riggio's biggest idea was that books appeal to most everyone, not just to intellectuals, writers, and students in cosmopolitan cities. Riggio listened to prospective customers who wanted bigger selections of books, more convenient locations, and less intimidating environments. He put superstores in all types of communities, from big cities like Atlanta and Chicago, to smaller cities like Midland, Texas, and Reno, Nevada. His respect for the customer led him to create stores with spacious and comfortable interiors, easy chairs for relaxing with a book, and Starbucks coffee bars. To this day, he considers his best decision the installation of easy-to-find public restrooms in the stores. As he said in a recent speech, "You work so hard and invest so much to get people to visit your store, why would you want them to have to leave?"

Besides the large selection of books, the stores also have an active calendar of author signings, poetry readings, children's events, and book discussion groups. Many Barnes & Noble superstores have become a social arena in which busy consumers—who normally rush in and out of other stores—linger.

Riggio sees the Internet as much more than a way to deliver books to customers; it's another opportunity to listen to them and thus show respect for them. He views the store network and Barnesandnoble.com as portals to each other. Customers can ask salespeople at Internet service counters to search Barnesandnoble.com for out-of-stock books, for customer reviews of titles that interest them, and for information about authors, such as other books they've published. Customers in a superstore can order the books they want on-line and have them shipped either to that store or to any other address. If a return is necessary, customers can bring their on-line purchase back to the store.

The value of respect often gets little more than lip service from retailers. Some companies wait until it's too late to put words into action.

Pillar 3: Connect with Your Customers' Emotions

Most retailers understand in principle that they need to connect emotionally with consumers; a good many don't

know how to (or don't try to) put the principle into practice. Instead, they neglect the opportunity to make emotional connections and put too much emphasis on prices.
The promise of low prices may appeal to customers' sense
of reason, but it does not speak to their passions.

Many U.S. furniture retailers are guilty of ignoring
consumers' emotions. Although the average size of new
homes in the country has grown by 25% since 1980, furniture accounts for a lower percentage of total U.S. consumer spending today (1%) than it did in 1980 (1.2%).
Making consumers wait up to two months to receive
their furniture contributes to these poor results. How
can consumers get emotionally involved in products they
know they won't see for weeks?

Poor marketing also hurts the industry. Most furniture stores focus strictly on price appeals, emphasizing
cost savings rather than the emotional lift that can come
from a new look in the home. "We don't talk about how
easy it can be to make your home more attractive," says
Jerry Epperson, an investment banker who specializes in
the furniture industry. "All we talk about is 'sale, sale,
sale' and credit terms."

Great retailers reach beyond the model of the rational
consumer and strive to establish feelings of closeness,
affection, and trust. The opportunity to establish such
feelings is open to any retailer, regardless of the type of
business or the merchandise being sold. Everyone is
emotionally connected to some retailers—from local
businesses such as the wine merchant who always
remembers what you like; to national companies like
Harley-Davidson, which connects people through its
Harley Owners Group; to catalog retailer Coldwater
Creek, which ships a substitute item to customers who
need to make returns before the original item is sent
back.

One retailer that has connected especially well with its target market in recent years is Journeys, a Nashville, Tennessee-based chain of shoe stores located primarily in shopping malls. The chain focuses on selling footwear to young men and women between the ages of 15 and 25. Started in 1987, Journeys didn't take off until 1995 when new management took over. The chain has achieved double-digit comparable-store sales increases in five of the six years since then and is now expanding by as many as 100 new stores per year.

Journeys has penetrated the skepticism and fickleness that are characteristic of many teens. By keeping a finger on the pulse of its target market, the company consistently has the right brands available for this especially brand-conscious group of consumers. Equally important, it creates the right store atmosphere—the stores pulsate with music, video, color, and brand merchandising.

A Journeys store is both welcoming and authentic to young people; it is simultaneously energetic and laid-back. Journeys' employees are typically young—the average age of a store manager is about 25—and they dress as they please. Customers frequently visit a store in groups just to hang out; salespeople exert no pressure to buy. And everyone, whether they've made a purchase or not, usually leaves with a giveaway—for instance, a key chain, a compact-disc case, a promotional T-shirt, or one of the 10 million or so stickers the stores give out over the course of a year. The stickers, which usually feature one of the brands Journeys sells, often end up on backpacks, skateboards, school lockers, or bathroom mirrors. Journeys also publishes a bimonthly magazine, *Dig,* that is available in the stores, and it runs a Web site that seeks to replicate the atmosphere of its stores. The number of site visits explodes whenever the company's commercials appear on MTV.

Journeys works in large part because it has created an atmosphere that connects emotionally with the young people it serves. Other retailers should bear in mind that it takes more than a room full of products with price tags on them to draw people in.

Connects Emotionally.

Pillar 4: Set the Fairest (Not the Lowest) Prices

Prices are about more than the actual dollars involved. If customers suspect that the retailer isn't playing fair, prices can also carry a psychological cost. Potential buyers will not feel comfortable making purchases if they fear that prices might be 30% lower next week, or if certain charges have only been estimated, or if they are unsure whether an advertised sale price represents a genuine markdown.

Consider some of the pricing tactics commonly used by certain home improvement retailers. One well-known company advertises products as "special buys" even though it has not lowered the regular prices. Another purposely misrepresents a competitor's prices on price-comparison signs within its stores. Still another company promotes lower-grade merchandise implying that it is top quality. One retailer puts a disclaimer in its ads that reads: "Prices in this ad may be different from the actual price at time of purchase. We adjust our prices daily to the lumber commodity market." The disclaimer paves the way for the retailer to raise its prices regardless of the advertised price.

Excellent retailers seek to minimize or eliminate the psychological costs associated with manipulative pricing. Most of these retailers follow the principles of "everyday fair pricing" instead of "everyday low pricing." A fact of retail life is that no retailer, not even

Wal-Mart, can truthfully promise customers that it will always have the lowest prices. An uncomfortable truth for many retailers is that their "lowest price anywhere" positioning is a crutch for the lack of value-adding innovation. Price is the only reason they give customers to care.

Retailers can implement a fair-pricing strategy by clearing two hurdles. First, they must make the cultural and strategic transition from thinking value equals price to realizing that value is the total customer experience. Second, they must understand the principles of fair pricing and muster the courage needed to put them into practice. Retailers who price fairly sell most goods at regular but competitive prices and hold legitimate sales promotions. They make it easy to compare their prices with those of competitors, and they avoid hidden charges. They don't raise prices to take advantage of temporary blips in demand, and they stand behind the products they sell.

Zane's Cycles in Branford, Connecticut, is one of the most successful independent bicycle retailers in the United States. Zane's has grown its one-store business at least 20% every year since it was founded in 1981, selling 4,250 bicycles in 2000 along with a full array of accessories. The company's success illustrates the appeal of fair pricing.

Zane's sells better bike brands with prices starting at $250. It stands behind what it sells with a 30-day test-drive offer (customers can return a bike within 30 days and exchange it for another) and a 90-day price protection guarantee (if a buyer finds the same bike in Connecticut at a lower price within 90 days, Zane's will refund the difference plus 10%). Zane's also offers free lifetime service on all new bicycles it sells; it was likely the first bicycle retailer in the United States to take this step. The promise of lifetime service includes annual tune-ups, brake and gear adjustments, wheel straightening, and more.

Zane's holds only one promotional sale a year, a three-day spring weekend event featuring discounts on all products. Vendors and former employees come to work at the huge event—some even fly in to participate. Customers who purchase a bicycle at Zane's within 90 days before the sale are encouraged to return during the event for a refund based on the discounted price of their bike. The company refunded about $3,000 during the 2000 sale, but most of that money remained in the store because customers bought more gear. Zane's sold 560 bicycles during the 2000 sale—that's more than the typical one-store U.S. bicycle retailer sells in an entire year. And yet the limited duration of the sale means that Zane's sells about 85% of its bicycles at the regular price.

When Connecticut passed a bike-helmet law in 1992, Zane's sold helmets to kids at cost rather than take advantage of legislated demand. Owner Chris Zane convinced area school administrators to distribute flyers to students under 12 announcing that policy. "We sold a ton of helmets and made a lot of new friends for the store," Zane says. "Our customers trust us. They come in and say, 'I am here to get a bike. What do I need?' They have confidence in our ability to find them just the right bike at a fair price and to stand behind what we sell."

Constant sales, markdowns on overinflated prices, and other forms of pressure pricing may boost sales in the short term. Winning customers' trust through fair pricing will pay off in the long term.

Pillar 5: Save Your Customers' Time

Many consumers are poor in at least one respect: they lack time. Retailers often contribute to the problem by wasting consumers' time and energy in myriad ways,

---

Are Your Retailing Pillars Solid—or Crumbling?

	Inferior retailers . . .	Superior retailers . . .
Solutions	gather products, stack them on shelves, put price tags on them, and wonder where their customers are.	consider what people really need and how they can meet that particular need better than competitors can.
Respect	are staffed by people who don't know what customers want and aren't about to interrupt their conversations to find out.	actually train and manage the salespeople they hire so that they are courteous, energetic, and helpful to customers.
Emotions	act as if their customers are Spock-like Vulcans who make purchases solely according to cold logic.	recognize that everything about a retail experience sends a message to customers that goes to the heart, not just the brain.
Pricing	focus exclusively on their supposed low prices, often because they have nothing else of value to offer customers.	focus on having fair prices instead of playing mind games with "special offers," fine print, and bogus sales.
Convenience	are open for business when it's convenient for them, close checkout lanes when it's convenient for them, deliver products when it's convenient for them, and so on.	understand that people's most precious commodity in the modern world is time and do everything they can to save as much of it as possible for their customers.

from confusing store layouts to inefficient checkout operations to inconvenient hours of business. When shopping is inconvenient, the value of a retailer's offerings plummets.

Slow checkout is particularly annoying to busy people. Managers usually know how much money they are saving by closing a checkout lane; but they may not realize how many customers they've lost in the process. For a food shopper waiting behind six other customers in the "10 Items or Fewer" lane to buy a carton of milk, the time invested in the purchase may outweigh the value of the milk. The shopper may follow through this time but find another store next time. Studies by America's Research Group, a consumer research company based in Charleston, South Carolina, indicate that 83% of women and 91% of men have ceased shopping at a particular store because of long checkout lines.

To compete most effectively, retailers must offer convenience in four ways. They must offer convenient retail locations and operating hours and be easily available by telephone and the Internet (access convenience). They must make it easy for consumers to identify and select desired products (search convenience). They need to make it possible for people to get the products they want by maintaining a high rate of in-stock items and by delivering store, Internet, or catalog orders swiftly (possession convenience). And they need to let consumers complete or amend transactions quickly and easily (transaction convenience).

ShopKo, a discount chain based in Green Bay, Wisconsin, illustrates how shopping speed and ease can create value. ShopKo's more than 160 large discount stores operate in 19 midwestern, mountain, and northwestern states; 80% of the customer base is working women.

With fiscal 1999 sales of $3.9 billion (including its small-market subsidiary, Pamida), ShopKo is much smaller than Wal-Mart, Kmart, or Target, yet it competes successfully against all three. Since 1995, following the arrival of new management a year earlier, ShopKo has more than doubled sales and achieved record earnings growth.

ShopKo takes possession convenience seriously and is in-stock 98% of the time on advertised and basic merchandise. Search convenience is another strength. ShopKo stores are remarkably clean and neat. Major traffic aisles are free of passage-blocking displays. Customers near the front of the store have clear sight lines to the back. Navigational signs hanging from the ceiling and on the ends of the aisles help point shoppers in the right direction. Clothing on a hanger has a size tag on the hanger neck; folded apparel has an adhesive strip indicating the size on the front of the garment. Children's garments have "simple sizing"—extra small, small, medium, and large—with posted signs educating shoppers on how to select the proper size.

ShopKo has a "one-plus-one" checkout policy of opening another checkout lane whenever two customers are waiting in any lane. Ready-to-assemble furniture is sold on a pull-tag system. The customer presents a coded tag at checkout and within three minutes the boxed merchandise is ready to be delivered to the customer's car. These ways of operating give ShopKo an edge in transaction convenience.

ShopKo is succeeding in the fiercely competitive discount sector by focusing on the total shopping experience rather than on having the lowest prices. Shopping speed and ease combined with a pleasant store atmosphere, a well-trained staff, and a carefully selected range of merchandise creates a strong mix of customer value.

While ShopKo creates real convenience for its customers, the term is often used carelessly in retailing. Consider that Internet shopping is commonly referred to as convenient. The Internet does indeed offer superior convenience for some stages of the shopping experience; it is inferior for other stages. On-line shoppers who save a trip to a physical store must wait for delivery. Christmas shoppers who receive gifts ordered on-line *after* the holiday learn a lesson about possession inconvenience. This is one reason that the most promising path for most retailers is a strategy that combines physical and virtual stores. Increasingly, the best-managed retailers will enable customers to take advantage of the most effective features of physical and virtual shopping, even for the same transaction.

RETAIL COMPETITION has never been more intense or more diverse than it is today. Yet the companies featured in this article, and hundreds of other excellent retailers, are thriving. They understand that neither technology nor promises of "the lowest prices anywhere" can substitute for a passionate focus on the total customer experience. These retailers enable customers to solve important problems, capitalize on the power of respectfulness, connect with customers' emotions, emphasize fair pricing, and save customers time and energy. In an age that demands instant solutions, it's not possible to combine those ingredients with Redi-Mix, crank out a concrete-block building, and hope the structure will stand. But retailers who thoughtfully and painstakingly erect these pillars will have a solid operation that is capable of earning customers' business, trust, and loyalty.

Originally published in April 2001
Reprint R0104J

Better Marketing at the Point of Purchase

JOHN A. QUELCH AND
KRISTINA CANNON-BONVENTRE

Executive Summary

RETAIL STORES have become the newest battleground in the war of consumer goods manufacturers to win customers. As advertising costs soar, retail sales efforts deteriorate, and consumers become more discriminating, manufacturers are discovering the need to reach potential buyers directly at the time and place at which the buying decision is made—the point of purchase. Manufacturers are finding that such tools as well-designed displays, distinctive packaging, price and sample promotions, and in-store advertising can provide them with a competitive edge. To make point-of-purchase programs work, manufacturers must be able not only to devise attractive displays but also to tailor them to various kinds of retail outlets. Finally, manufacturers must effectively execute their programs by clearly delineating their responsibilities vis-à-vis those of their retailers and by choosing the best means of servicing them.

THE RETAIL POINT of purchase represents the time and place at which all the elements of the sale—the consumer, the money, and the product—come together. By using various communications vehicles, including displays, packaging, sales promotions, in-store advertising, and salespeople, at the point of purchase (POP), the marketer hopes to influence the consumer's buying decision.

Partly because of the diversity of communications vehicles available and partly because effective POP programs can aid in competing for retailers' support, marketers need to manage their POP programs carefully so as to ensure that both retailers and consumers will see consistency and coordination in the programs rather than confusion and contradiction. Recent examples of innovative, well-managed POP programs include:

- Atari's Electronic Retail Information Center (ERIC), a computerized display installed in more than 500 stores that is designed to help sell computers. An Atari 800 home computer linked to a videodisk player asks a series of questions to help the retailer determine a customer's level of computer ability and product needs. ERIC then switches on a video disk that plays the most appropriate of 13 messages based on the customer's inputs.[1]

- Kodak's Disc Camera, launched in May 1982. A rotating display unit presented the disc story to the consumer without the need for salesperson assistance. In addition to the display unit, the POP program included merchandising aids, sales training and meetings for retail store personnel, film display and dispenser units, giant film cartoons, window streamers, lapel buttons, and cash register display cards.[2]

• Ford Motor Company's showroom wine-and-cheese parties, started in Dallas and San Diego in 1982 to provide a "more comfortable [car] buying process for women" and to respond to the fact that 40% of new car purchases (valued at $35 billion) are now made by women. The auto showroom has traditionally been an uncomfortable environment for women, whom salesmen have often patronized or overpowered with technical details. The showroom events represent an effort to manage the point of purchase to attract an increasingly important customer segment.[3]

Innovative management of the point of purchase has been applied to a broad range of consumer product categories, including:

• Candy, gum, and magazines, which depend on impulse purchases for a large percentage of their sales.

• Personal computers and other new technical products that require in-store demonstration.

• Pantyhose and vitamins, which because they include multiple items in each brand line must be presented especially clearly to the consumer and efficiently stocked.

• Lawn and garden appliances, which are sold through several types of retailers, each of whom requires a different POP program.

- Liquor and tobacco, which are prohibited from advertising in some media.

- Automobiles and other mature, large-ticket items usually associated with intensive personal selling.

We believe that the expenditures of consumer goods manufacturers on POP communications will increase and that marketers who can manage events at the point of purchase well can gain competitive advantage. In this article we consider why managing the point of purchase is becoming more important, the roles of each element of the POP communications mix, and how consumer goods marketers can improve their management of the point of purchase.

POP's New Importance

POP expenditures are of increasing significance to marketers for three reasons. First, they often prove more productive than advertising and promotion expenditures. Second, the decline in sales support at the store level is stimulating interest among retailers in manufacturers' POP programs. Third, changes in consumers' shopping patterns and expectations, along with an upsurge in impulse buying, mean that the point of purchase is playing a more important role in consumers' decision making than ever before.

For the same reasons, retailers are becoming increasingly receptive to manufacturers' offers of POP merchandising programs. Even K mart stores, long off limits to manufacturers' sales representatives, now allow them to set up displays and offer planograms. The delicate power balance between the manufacturer and the trade is such, however, that retailers will not give up control of the

POP readily, particularly at a time when its importance is growing. Moreover, the pressure on retailers to carve out distinctive positionings to survive heightens their determination to control store layouts, space allocations, and POP merchandising.

Hence, at the same time that their interest in manufacturers' POP programs is rising, retailers are becoming more selective than they once were and beginning to impose constraints, such as restricting the height of displays to preserve the vistas in each department and on each floor. To maintain consistency in store formats and to take advantage of volume discounts, Sears, Roebuck and Company recently centralized all fixture ordering at headquarters.

IMPROVING COMMUNICATIONS PRODUCTIVITY

Marketers are carefully examining alternatives and supplements to media advertising, which has roughly tripled in cost since 1968. POP programs cannot substitute for media advertising, nor are they as easily controlled in the store since they are implemented on someone else's turf. They can, however, reinforce and remind consumers about the advertising messages they have seen before entering the store. POP programs help improve productivity in the following ways:

Low cost. While reaching 1,000 adults through a 30-second network television commercial costs $4.05 to $7.75, the cost per thousand for a store merchandiser or a sign with a one-year life is only 3 cents to 37 cents.[4] These figures reflect the low production and installation costs of POP materials and the fact that the same POP materials are seen repeatedly by consumers and salespeople.

Consumer focus. POP programs focus on the consumer but also provide a service to the trade. Because they help move products off the shelves into consumers' hands, POP expenditures are often more productive than off-invoice price reductions to the trade, which risk being pocketed and therefore withheld from the consumer.

Precise target marketing. POP programs can be easily tailored to the needs of local markets or classes of trade in response to marketers' increasing emphasis on region-by-region marketing programs and on account management of key retail customers. In addition, particular consumer segments can be precisely targeted. Revlon's Polished Ambers Dermanesse Skin programmer, a non-electronic teaching aid used at the point of purchase to suggest appropriate cosmetic combinations to black women, exemplifies a targeted approach that could not be undertaken efficiently via media advertising alone.

Easy evaluation. Alternative POP programs can be inexpensively presented in split samples of stores. Stores equipped with check-out scanner systems can quickly provide the sales data needed to evaluate the impact of POP programs for the benefit of both manufacturer and retailer.

DECLINING RETAIL SALES PUSH

Manufacturers are increasingly questioning whether they can rely on retail sales clerks to push their products at the point of purchase. The quality of retail salespeople appears to have declined as their status has diminished. Their high turnover rate (often more than 100% per year) reflects their relatively low educational level and remuneration.

Sales positions are increasingly being viewed as dead-end jobs since more retailers now prefer to hire university-trained managers.

To reduce labor costs and remain price competitive, retailers such as Sears have cut the number of clerks covering the floor in favor of centralized checkouts. Consumers have developed the impression that salespeople are less attentive and knowledgeable when, in fact, they have to cover more shoppers and product lines than before.

To cut costs while extending opening hours, retailers have also shifted to inexperienced and uncommitted part-time salespersons, who often know little about a product's features and cannot demonstrate its use.

Thus, retail salespeople increasingly lack both ability and credibility. Effective POP programs can compensate for such sales weaknesses by enabling the manufacturer to maintain control of the message delivered to the consumer at the place and time of the final purchase decision. Marketers who provide the most attractive, educational, entertaining, and easy-to-use POP programs are likely to win the favor of store management. Their products are also likely to receive more push from overextended retail salespeople because an effective POP program can increase their credibility and facilitate the selling task.

CHANGING CONSUMER EXPECTATIONS

These days consumers are inclined to seek special deals and wait for sales before they buy large ticket items or stock up on small items. As a result, consumer demand for such products as cosmetics and home furnishings fluctuates more widely than ever before. Retailers are interested in POP merchandising techniques and displays that can productively occupy consumers while they are waiting for sales help. For this reason and because of union restrictions on part-time personnel, Bell Phone Centers, for example, offer consumers many POP aids, including demonstration units.

The increasing use of automatic teller machines and vending machines, the expanded use of self-service store formats, and the advent of computerized shopping mall guides all indicate that consumers who value speed and convenience are becoming amenable to helping themselves at the point of purchase. This trend is evident, for example, in hardware stores, where manufacturers such as McCulloch and retail chains such as ServiStar are providing more and more display centers to present their product lines.

Many consumers wish to do their shopping quickly and efficiently; yet, at the same time, the longer they are in a retail store, the more likely they are to buy. Purchases planned least often were, according to one survey, auto supplies (94%), magazines and newspapers (91%), and candy and gum (85%).[5] Drugstore purchases, too, were largely unplanned—60% of them, including 78% of snack food and 69% of cosmetics purchases.[6] An average of 39% of department store purchases were unplanned, ranging from 27% of women's lingerie purchases to 62% of costume jewelry purchases.[7] Effective POP programs not only present useful information efficiently; they can also make shopping entertaining and remove some of its frustration.

The Point-of-Purchase Communications Mix

How can consumer goods marketers address the different—and sometimes conflicting—interests of the manufacturer, the retailer, and the consumer at the point of purchase?

USING DISPLAYS EFFECTIVELY

For one thing, they can use well-designed displays. They attract consumer attention, facilitate product inspection and selection, allow the access of several shoppers at once, inform and entertain, and stimulate unplanned expenditures. Because additional display space can expand sales without any change in retail price, consumer goods marketers increased their spending on POP displays 12% annually between 1980 and 1982. Well-designed displays respond to the needs of both the retailer and the consumer.

They reduce store labor costs by facilitating shelf stocking and inventory control, minimizing out-of-stock items, and lowering the required level of back-room inventory. For example, automatic feed displays such as 7-Up's single-can dispensers eliminate the need for store clerks to realign shelf stock.

Good displays are designed for a particular type of store and often for a specific store department. For example, the Entenmann Division of General Foods realized that its display designs in the bakery sections of supermarkets were not transferable to the cash register areas, where the company wished to sell its new line of snacks, so it developed an additional range of displays.

Good displays reflect the likely level of trade support. There is no point in designing a large display that will not generate the retailer's required level of inventory turnover. Likewise, there is no point in offering the trade a permanent display for a seasonal product. Richardson-Vicks, for example, redesigns its display each year rather than provide a permanent fixture because retailers give floor space to Vicks Cold Centers during the winter months only.

Well-designed displays are versatile and can accommodate new products. Max Factor, for example, provides retailers with a floor-stand display consisting of a series of interchangeable trays and cartridges. New product lines, packed in similar trays, can be easily inserted, while the cartridges can, when removed from the floor stand, double as counter display units.

Manufacturers must, of course, also keep their own interests in mind when they are designing displays. For example, Johnson & Johnson's First Aid Center provides supermarkets and drugstores with a permanent display for more than 30 of its first aid items.[8] By creating a strong visual impact at the point of purchase, the display presents Johnson & Johnson as a large, well-established company that offers consumers the convenience of easy product selection and "one-shelf shopping" for all their first aid needs. It also discourages retailers from stocking only the fastest-moving items. In addition, the display carries the company name and thus prevents the retailers from using the display to stock other products. At the same time, it helps Johnson & Johnson preempt competition in slow-moving product categories in which the retailer can justify stocking only one brand.

While displays such as these are becoming prevalent in self-service environments, other innovative displays are being developed to supplement the efforts of salespeople. For example, Mannington Mills' Compu-Flor, a small computerized display placed in floor covering retail outlets, is programmed to use a potential consumer's answers to eight questions about room decor. The terminal then displays three to ten appropriate Mannington styles for the customer to choose from. When idle, the machine beeps periodically to attract consumers. Mannington had placed the units in 700 stores by the end of 1982 at a cost of $8 million, an amount equal to the company's advertising budget.

Mannington found that Compu-Flor selected styles for customers more efficiently than salespeople (who had trouble remembering all the styles in the product line), encouraged salespeople to push Mannington products rather than those of its two larger competitors (Armstrong and Congoleum), and boosted the number of sales closed on a customer's first store visit.[9]

Compu-Flor is just one of a number of computerized video displays at the point of purchase that provide a standard controllable message from manufacturer to consumer, a way of engaging customers' attention while they are waiting for sales assistance, and entertainment.

A PACKAGE IS MORE THAN A CONTAINER

Packaging has many functions beyond acting as a container for a product.

Appropriate packaging, of course, attracts attention at the point of purchase. Manufacturers such as Nabisco and Kellogg use the same package design for many items in their product lines to present a highly visible billboard of packages to consumers at the point of purchase. In 1979, Nabisco standardized the package design of its chocolate-covered cookies; the market share for this product rose from 24% to 34% by 1981.[10]

Standardized packaging also permits easy identification of brands, types, and sizes. Private-label suppliers have imitated the color codes used to identify various sizes of disposable diapers made by the brand name manufacturers. Similarly, packaging communicates product benefits and identifies target groups. Contrast the packaging of Marlboro cigarettes, aimed at men, Virginia Slims, targeted at women, and Benson & Hedges Deluxe Ultra Lights, with a silver package designed to appeal to elitists among both men and women.

And the right packaging limits the potential for pilferage of small items. The manufacturer of Fevertest, a plastic strip that, when placed on the forehead, indicates the presence of fever, added size and value to the product by enclosing the strip in a wallet, packaging the wallet in a blister pack, and displaying the item on pegboards at supermarket and drugstore checkout counters.

Consumer and trade expectations of product packaging should not discourage marketers from innovation, though frequent changes in package size and design breed trade resistance, especially when existing shelf configurations cannot easily accommodate the new packages. Reflecting the shift to self-service car maintenance, Kendall and Arco recently began to sell oil in plastic containers with built-in pouring spouts.

MAKING SHOPPING FUN

Manufacturers are increasingly using consumer promotions to make shopping exciting. These include premiums, coupons, samples, and refund offers in or on product packages to help them stand out and break through the visual clutter at the point of purchase. Package-delivered promotions have the further advantage of being inexpensive in comparison with consumer promotions offered in magazine advertisements or direct mail campaigns.

Manufacturers are also becoming aware that retailers favor manufacturers whose promotions bring consumers into the store. For example, some sweepstakes promotions, such as Brown Shoe Company's Footworks contest, encourage the consumer to match symbols in an advertisement with those on a store display or package in order to enter the contest. Retailers also like promotions that tie into store merchandising themes and cross-sell other products (promotions built around recipes or complete home decorating services, for instance) and promotions that avoid the use of special price packs that require retailers to replace existing shelf stock and set up new Universal Product Code entries in store computer systems.

IN-STORE ADVERTISING MEDIA

Manufacturers can extend to retailers a number of innovative approaches for reinforcing brand awareness and delivering advertising messages at the point of purchase. These include:

Commercials broadcast over in-store sound systems.

Moving message display units with changeable electronic messages.

Customer-activated videotapes and video disks that show merchandise such as furniture that is too bulky to be displayed on the department floor; the videotapes can also be played in window displays to present, for example, designer fashion shows.

Television sets installed over cash registers to show waiting customers commercials for products that are usually available nearby.

Advertisements on carts used in supermarkets and other self-service outlets.

Danglers and mobile displays that use available air space rather than limited floor space.

Implementation Steps

Recognizing the significance of the point of purchase is not enough. Consumer goods marketers must pay more attention to developing effective POP programs and, even more important, to ensuring that they are properly implemented at the store level.

Before developing a POP program, managers must have a clear understanding of their marketing strategy—which products are being delivered to which markets through which channels of distribution. Given the marketing strategy, marketers should go on to answer such questions as:

What must happen at the point of purchase to satisfy consumer needs?

Which channel members—manufacturers, retailers, consumers—are willing to perform which functions?

Which members can perform them most cost-effectively?

How should the functions be allocated?

How should the pricing structure for the product (and for the POP program) reflect this allocation of functions?

PROGRAM DEVELOPMENT

Once they answer these questions, marketers can work out the specifics of the POP program—objectives, vehicles, and budgets. Here are five principles that should guide this process:

1. Integrate all elements of the POP communications mix. The package, for example, cannot be designed independently of the display. All POP vehicles should communicate consistent and mutually reinforcing messages to both the trade and the consumer.

2. Offer the trade a coordinated POP program for an entire product line rather than a collection of POP materials for particular items. To further impress the trade, make sure that the POP program is easy to understand and financially realistic.

3. Link POP assistance to trade performance. High-quality displays, for example, should not be given away to the trade unless linked to a quantity purchase or paid for with cooperative advertising dollars earned on previous purchases.

4. Assume that various POP programs will be necessary for distribution channels. The traditional hardware store and the self-service mass merchandiser, for example, differ both in store environment and in type of customer; the ideal POP program for each will not be the same.

5. Integrate POP communications with non-POP communications. Television advertising should tell consumers in which stores and departments they can find the advertised product and should include shots of product packages and displays to facilitate consumer recall and brand identification at the point of purchase. Sometimes a POP display becomes the basis for a television advertising campaign, as in the case of the Uniroyal POP unit, which invited the

consumer to drill a hole in a Royal Seal tire to demonstrate that no air was lost if it was punctured.

PROGRAM EXECUTION

Any POP program is only as effective as the quality of its implementation at the store level. Effective implementation requires that managers, first, recognize the execution challenge. Many innovative approaches to managing the point of purchase fail because responsibilities for such tasks as stocking and maintaining displays are not clearly allocated or, once allocated, are not properly performed. Under these circumstances, cooperation between manufacturers and retailers can quickly turn into recrimination.

Consumer goods marketers are often too eager to assume POP responsibilities themselves. To increase their control over the execution of their marketing programs, they might enhance effectiveness and reduce expense to make the programs work by appropriately compensating the retailers.

Two recent examples highlight the risks of ineffective execution at the point of purchase:

- General Entertainment Corporation failed in its 1982 attempt to market popular music cassette tapes from floor-stand displays in supermarkets partly because its field sales force could not maintain display inventories of 168 stockkeeping units, many of which changed every few months.

- Binney & Smith, manufacturer of Crayola crayons and other arts materials, quickly placed 1,500 special merchandising units called Crayola Fun Centers in a variety of distribution outlets following their introduction in 1980. But efficiently servicing the displays proved difficult, and Binney terminated the contract of the servicing firm handling this task.

In general, the greater the number of stockkeeping units in a display and the greater the diversity of channel environments in which the displays are placed, the more complex and challenging effective execution becomes.

Next, managers must evaluate the execution alternatives. Consumer goods marketers usually have three options for carrying out POP programs—to use their own salespeople, to contract with brokers or service merchandisers, and to rely on the retailer. The evaluation should center on comparative costs, degree of marketers' control over the execution, and the relative importance of effective POP merchandising in leveraging a product's overall marketing program. The more important it is, the more justification the marketer has for using a direct sales force.

One important reason for the success of L'eggs was the company's decision to have its own salespeople deliver the product on consignment to stores and to assume total responsibility for managing the point of purchase. Yet the ability of the L'eggs salespeople to stock product displays efficiently had a negative twist; although it enabled L'eggs to introduce numerous line extensions, their addition complicated the product selection process at the point of purchase and made it seem inconvenient in the minds of many consumers.

To ensure the freshness and integrity of its snacks, Frito-Lay's 9,000 van salespeople visit 300,000 outlets each week. Beyond taking orders, they are trained to advise retailers about how to allocate shelf space in the snack food section according to a six-point space management program. Yet, despite the clout of its sales force, Frito-Lay could not persuade supermarkets to stock its new line of Grandma's cookies at supermarket check-out counters; they are now being displayed in the cookie sections.

These two examples deliver an important message. Even when a company has the sales force to ensure the execution of a POP program, it must never lose sight of the needs of consumers and the trade.

Many consumer goods marketers cannot afford their own sales forces and must rely on brokers or service merchandisers. Both are often unfairly demeaned. A good broker is sometimes more effective than a direct sales force in managing the point of purchase, as many big companies, including H. J. Heinz and Pillsbury, know well. Because they carry a number of noncompeting product lines, brokers enjoy economies of scale that enable them to visit retail stores more often than a manufacturer's sales force to check stocks, reset displays, and offer planograms. Brokers can establish close relationships with retailers in their local areas and organize blockbuster promotional events for their principals. For frozen food manufacturers, brokers are especially important to managing the point of purchase. Frequent store visits are essential because freezer space is limited on account of equipment and energy costs, and stores carry little, if any, back-room inventory.

If your company uses brokers or service merchandisers, here are four approaches to ensure that they effectively execute your POP program:

1. Check the size of the broker's sales force against the company's product line commitments. Is the broker-

age firm overextended? How important is your business to the firm?

2. Develop a POP program that is creative yet easy to implement. As a result, your company may gain more attention from the broker's sales people (and, therefore, the trade) than the broker's other principals.

3. Compensate the broker appropriately for the POP tasks you expect him or her to perform. Do you provide bonus incentives to broker salespeople for additional display placements?

4. Evaluate POP performance. Do you buy display audits to compare your share of display space with your market share? Do you occasionally play the customer, visit stores, check displays, and ask sales clerks for information?

T HESE SAME PRINCIPLES are relevant whether the retailer, a broker, or a direct sales force is responsible for executing the POP program. The most important point for the consumer goods marketer to recognize is that an effective POP program never runs like clockwork. It needs constant attention and reevaluation.

Many consumer goods marketers are increasing their expenditures on POP programs. In 1982, for example, Elizabeth Arden, Inc. raised its POP budget by 40%.[11] What these marketers recognize is the old adage that the difference between success and failure often depends on the last 5% of effort rather than on the 95% that preceded it. In consumer marketing, that last 5% manifests itself at the point of purchase just before consumers choose what to buy.

Notes

1. "Firms Start Using Computers to Take the Place of Salesmen," *Wall Street Journal*, July 15, 1982.

2. "Kodak's Dazzling Disc Introduction," *Marketing Communications*, July 1982, p. 21.

3. "Wine, Baubles, and Glamor Are Used to Help Lure Female Consumers to Ford's Showrooms," *Marketing News*, August 6, 1982, p. 1.

4. "Consumer Product Marketing: The Role of Permanant Point-of-Purchase," *POPAI News*, vol. 6, no. 2, 1982, p. 5.

5. "POPAI/Dupont Consumer Buying Habits Survey," *Chain Store Age/Supermarkets*, December 1978, p. 41.

6. "Store Buying Decisions: 60 Percent In-Store," *POPAI News*, vol. 6, no. 2, 1982, p. 1.

7. D. N. Bellenger, D. H. Robertson, and E. C. Hirschman, "Impulse Buying Varies by Product," *Journal of Advertising Research*, vol. 18, 1978, p. 15.

8. "Marketing Textbook: Case History J&J First Aid Shelf Management System," *POPAI News*, vol. 6, no. 2, 1982, p. 8.

9. Lawrence Stevens, "A Computer to Help Salesmen Sell," *Personal Computing*, November 1982, p. 62.

10. Don Veraska, "More Than One Tough Cookie Wrapped This One Up," *Advertising Age*, August 9, 1982, p. M-14.

11. "A Facelift for Elizabeth Arden," *Business Week*, August 23, 1982, p. 101.

Originally published in November–December 1983
Reprint 83614

Rocket Science Retailing Is Almost Here

Are You Ready?

MARSHALL L. FISHER, ANANTH RAMAN,
AND ANNA SHEEN MCCLELLAND

Executive Summary

DESPITE ALL THE DATA that retailers and e-tailers can now gather about point-of-purchase information, buying patterns, and customers' tastes, they still haven't figured out how to offer the right product, in the right place, at the right time, for the right price.

Most retailers largely ignore the billions of bytes of customer data stored in their databases—or they handle that information incorrectly. As a result, they don't adequately supply what consumers demand.

But some retailers are moving profitably toward what the authors call "rocket science retailing"—a blend of traditional forecasting systems, which are largely based on the gut feel of employees, with the prowess of information technology.

Marshall Fisher, Ananth Raman, and Anna Sheen McClelland recently finished surveying 32 retail

companies in which they tracked their practices and
progress in four areas critical to rocket science retailing:
demand forecasting, supply-chain speed, inventory planning, and data gathering and organization.

In this article, the authors look at some companies
that have excelled in those four areas and offer some
valuable advice for other businesses seeking retailing
perfection. In particular, the authors emphasize the need
to monitor crucial metrics such as forecast accuracy,
early sales data, and stockouts—information that will
help retailers determine when to tweak their supply-chain
processes to get the right products to stores at just the
right time.

The authors discuss the information technologies now
available for tracking that information. They point out the
flaws in some reporting and planning systems and suggest alternate methods for measuring stockouts, inventory, and losses.

THE HOLY GRAIL OF RETAILING—being able to
offer the right product in the right place at the right time
for the right price—remains frustratingly elusive. You
would think we'd have captured it by now, particularly
given the enormous amount of data that retailers and
e-tailers can gather about points of purchase, buying patterns, and customers' tastes. But many retailers still have
a long way to go.

Witness the much-publicized problems that e-tailers
have had delivering the products that customers order
on their Web sites. And who hasn't gone to a store only
to find that it doesn't have the right item—even though
the place is loaded with inventory, mostly discounted

goods? Department store markdowns have grown from 8% of store sales in 1971 to 33% in 1995. These numbers include promotional markdowns as well as the forced markdowns that are the result of manufacturers' over-supply. But the increase is so large that most observers take it as a sign that retailers are having a hard time matching supply with demand.

That's not to say progress hasn't been made. Some retailers (we'll refer to retailers and e-tailers henceforth with the broader term) have dramatically improved their performance in ordering, distribution, and merchandising. But those companies are still a small, elite rank. The next step? An industrywide move toward something we call rocket science retailing—the act of blending traditional forecasting systems, which are largely based on the intuition of a handful of employees, with the prowess of information technology. Rocket science retailing fuses data and instinct with computer models and analysis to create a high-tech forecasting system supported by a flexible supply chain.

The model is not as far-fetched as you might think. Wall Street went through just such a transformation in the 1970s. (See the sidebar "It Happened on Wall Street" at the end of this article.) And we've seen many retailers come quite close to achieving rocket science status during the past three years, as we've studied how they gather and process information, how they forecast demand, and how they manage their supplier relationships.

We recently completed an in-depth, multiyear survey of 32 generally cutting-edge companies in which we tracked their practices and progress in four areas critical to achieving rocket science retailing: forecasting, supply-chain speed, inventory planning, and gathering accurate, available data. In this article, we'll illustrate what some companies are doing best in these four areas, with the hope that other retailers can use their insights and practices to gain ground on the grail.

Forecasting

For many of the retailers in our study, forecasting product demand is a right-brain function that relies on the gut feel of a few individuals and not on the systematic use of sales data. But it's a big mistake to overlook the opportunity to mix art and science. Retailers can significantly improve forecast accuracy simply by updating their predictions based on early sales data, tracking the accuracy of their forecasts, getting product testing right, and using a variety of forecasting approaches. Let's discuss each of these practices.

UPDATE FORECASTS BASED ON EARLY SALES DATA

Early product sales, appropriately adjusted for variations in price and availability, are an excellent predictor of overall sales (see the exhibit "No Need for a Crystal Ball"). In fact, retailers that exploit these data for production and inventory planning can more than double their profits—especially retailers of products with short life cycles, such as clothing, consumer electronics, books, and music.

But despite the potentially high payoff—and a commonly accepted belief among retailers that early sales are a good indicator of future sales—many of the companies we surveyed had no systems in place to exploit early sales data. One retailer, for example, ordered garments and committed specific quantities of each stock-keeping

No Need for a Crystal Ball

Early sales data can help to predict demand for the life cycle of a product–particularly a fashion item. The information below is from an apparel catalog company. The graph on the left plots actual life cycle demand against the forecasts made by a committee of four merchandisers. The graph on the right plots actual life cycle demand against forecasts based on sales observed during the product's first two weeks on the market, which accounted for 11% of the season's demand. The latter results in a forecast margin of error that is significantly less than the experts' forecast.

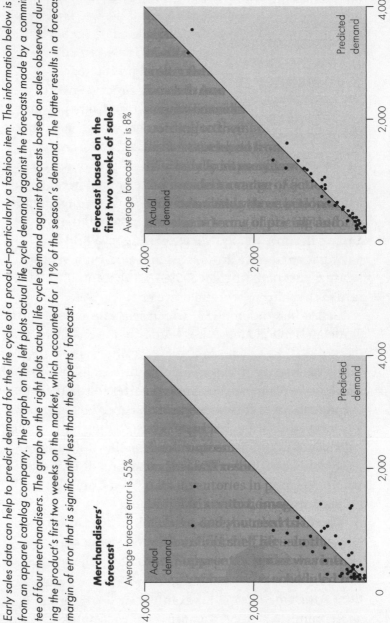

Merchandisers' forecast

Average forecast error is 55%

Forecast based on the first two weeks of sales

Average forecast error is 8%

unit (SKU) to each of its stores 11 months before the product was even available to the public. Even retailers that paid attention to their early sales data updated their forecasts in an ad hoc manner when sales greatly exceeded or fell far short of original predictions.

Several companies have retailing practices worth emulating, however. Japan-based World Company and Spain-based Zara are fashion retailers whose merchants systematically examine early sales data to estimate future demand for various products. They conduct this analysis for every product at predetermined periods in its sales cycle. And the merchants follow through, immediately reordering items that look as though they may end up in short supply. Not surprisingly, World Company has achieved a gross-margin return on inventory investments of more than 300%—a substantially higher return than any other retailer we are aware of.

Dallas-based CompUSA, which sells computers and associated merchandise, has found that even one or two days of early sales data can be very useful to predict sales and replenish its inventory for PCs. Buyers monitor the sales of a certain product line soon after it is launched and update their forecasts based on those observations. They expedite orders for PCs that are selling better than expected and, when possible, they decline items that have not been shipped. This process of reading and reacting to market signals has improved CompUSA's ability to match supply with demand.

Finally, book and music retailer Borders Group uses historical sales data to customize the product assortment in each of its stores. Borders tracks sales at each store by product category. It uses its merchandise planning system to automatically adjust the inventory at a store based on sales in each product category. Thus, a store in Anchorage, Alaska, would carry a wide assortment of books about small planes because sales for such books tend to be high at that outlet, while the Boston store might stock relatively few items in this category because demand is lower there. Why don't more retailers customize their inventories? The answer, as we explain later on, lies in slow supply chains, inadequate or inaccurate data, the inability to measure stockouts and forecast error, and planning software that is inappropriate for the retailer.

TRACK AND PREDICT FORECAST ACCURACY

Only nine of the 32 retailers in our study said they analyzed the accuracy of their forecasts. And yet, tracking forecast errors, and understanding when and why they occur, is fundamental to improving accuracy. Even more important, knowing the margin of error on a forecast is vital to being able to react when the forecast is wrong. For example, if past forecasts for a certain product have been wrong by plus or minus 50%, when a merchant says you'll sell 10,000 of that item, that really means you'll sell between 5,000 and 15,000 units. Instead of buying 10,000, it might be smarter to buy 5,000 finished units and materials for an additional 10,000 units to be assembled quickly if early sales are strong.

World Company tracks and predicts forecast accuracy by item using the "Obermeyer method": new products are displayed in a room at corporate headquarters just as they would be in a retail store, and about 30 store employees, who are chosen to represent the company's target customers, estimate the likely success of each product. World has found that the products that generate greater disagreement among the employees are likely to have less-accurate forecasts.

GET THE PRODUCT TESTING RIGHT

An impressive 78% of the retailers in our study test new products in a few stores before the actual product launch. But almost all the buyers said their test methods are highly unscientific and that any results that indicate that certain products will be *unsuccessful* are often ignored. Merchants often believe their products will sell well despite unfavorable test results; they blame the weather (bad or good), the poor choice of test sites, the inferior execution of tests, and other factors for sub-optimal sales.

When a product testing method is developed with care and refined on a regular basis, the results can substantially improve forecasts. We helped develop a testing method at one apparel retailer that predicts the sales of a product based on the early sales at a few carefully selected test stores. We found that the selection of stores greatly affected the quality of the forecasts. By using historical sales data to pick a diverse group of test stores that matched varying customer preferences, we reduced forecast errors for each style and color from 30% to 9%.

USE A VARIETY OF
FORECASTING APPROACHES

Most companies we surveyed limit themselves to just one type of forecasting. Generally, a single forecast for each item is generated by the buyer or by a small group from merchandising. But generating multiple forecasts can be very valuable because in seeking to understand the differences in those forecasts, managers can explore the assumptions implicit in their forecasting techniques.

Take Old Navy, a division of the Gap. The company blends bottom-up and top-down forecasting approaches and then considers the results in a way worth emulating. Bottom-up forecasts are developed by merchandisers and planners who predict demand for each product based on factors such as current trends in the market, the product's "fit" with the target customer, and the complementary products that will also be offered. Top-down forecasts are developed by planners and occur independent of the bottom-up process. They are based on macroeconomic factors such as the economic growth rate and corporate growth objectives. The two approaches typically yield different results, which are reconciled during a meeting of managers from both groups. Old Navy finds that the different processes, and the ensuing discussion, lead to substantially better forecasts.

Supply-Chain Speed

Many products today have such long lead times that retailers can't call for a change in production—even if they have tracked early sales, have paid attention to product testing, and know without a doubt that a change is warranted. As one merchant told us, "We do pay attention to our tests. The problem is we already own the product; the test merely reveals that it will be a dog once it gets to the stores." Another retailer maintains an 11-month lead time from placing an order to receiving apparel at the distribution center—even for products with a life cycle of only three months. Consequently, buyers have to commit to ordering from a single vendor before any sales data are obtained. They must also specify how much of each product will be delivered to each store 11 months before the material is received at the distribution center.

Supply-chain speed is clearly a critical component of rocket science retailing, particularly for products that have short life cycles. A company that can observe early sales and respond quickly with any appropriate additional merchandise can obviously reduce the likelihood of selling out of hot items. It can also reduce markdowns because its ability to respond with more products during the season means the retailer can order less initially and cut its losses on products that turn out to be failures.

World and Zara use similar exemplary practices in this area. Consider how World manages its supply chain. It can manufacture and deliver an existing product to stores in two weeks. It can design a new product and supply it to stores in as little as three weeks. How does the company achieve such short response times? First, World does a considerable amount of work with supply chain partners before it even places an order. The company stores fabrics and findings (buckles, zippers, and so on) and reserves production capacity at factories in anticipation of demand. At the beginning of a sales season, World, like most retailers, finds it difficult to predict the sales of each product. It knows that carrying an inventory of finished products is risky. But the company does find it relatively safe to hold raw-material inventory and reserve production capacity, since forecasts for those materials tend to be more accurate than forecasts for finished products.

Second, World's factories troubleshoot production problems—separate from the main manufacturing area.

The employees in the "debug area" work closely with designers at World's corporate office, changing the product design to enable easier manufacturing and, at times, replacing hard-to-find raw materials with more easily available materials.

Third, World has empowered its employees in product design, merchandising, operations, and its stores to make some decisions on their own, thus avoiding the bureaucratic delays that can accompany the decision-making process. For example, the decision to design, price, procure materials for, and manufacture a new product at World usually involves a meeting of five or six division managers who work in adjacent offices as a cross-functional team. At other retailers, such a meeting might involve convening managers located in different cities and might mean getting approval from executives at various levels in the organization—a more time-consuming process.

Why aren't other retailers as responsive as World? One common problem at many companies is an "efficiency mentality." The apparel retailer with the 11-month product lead time, for example, insisted on placing orders for individual stores instead of buying in bulk for all the stores and then strategically allocating goods to different stores once materials arrived at the distribution center. The retailer reduced its transportation costs and its inventory carrying costs at the warehouse, but it limited its ability to react quickly to market signals.

One distribution center manager told us about a video his company had produced illustrating how distribution efficiency could be improved. The video showed how fast warehouse personnel could gather garments for shipment if they collected and packed the reorders in the same mix of sizes—regardless of how many large, medium, and small items an individual store needed. The video also showed how much longer it took the warehouse staffers to collect the orders when the size mix for each store varied according to its need. The distribution manager and his peers were confident that the few-seconds-per-garment time savings would convince store managers that all reorders should be shipped in identical size mixes. Which begged our question to the manager: "How long does it take you to process garments that come back from the stores unsold because you haven't shipped what they need?"

Many retailers fall into a vicious cycle. Logistics and procurement officials argue that reducing lead times for products won't help the retailer because the company lacks good sales data and the tools to analyze that data. Merchandise-planning officials argue that being able to store and analyze sales data won't help the retailer since logistics and procurement can't respond fast enough to those signals. The problem is that companies can't quantify the value of a short lead time in reducing stockouts and markdowns. But as retailers adopt new software tools for forecasting and planning supply, they can use these tools to measure the impact of a shorter lead time and to better match supply with demand.

Inventory Planning

Inventory planning involves deciding when and how much to order, or how much to produce, of various raw materials, components, and finished goods. Inventory planning differs from forecasting because a planner might find it beneficial to stock more or less than predicted demand. In planning inventory for a household, for example, you might decide to stock far more medicine than you anticipate needing in case you become sick. Or you might buy certain items—batteries, for instance—many months' demand at a time while other items—bread and milk, for instance—might be ordered every week. Inventory planning at most retailers suffers from several shortcomings. One of the most glaring is that many retailers don't track stockouts and the resulting lost sales. Only 13 of the 32 companies in our study said they track stockouts, and 11 of the 13 used this information to estimate the resulting lost sales.

Lost sales are endemic among retailers, especially for products with short life cycles. Tracking stockouts could help retailers set optimal inventory levels and could help them see the value in improving supply-chain responsiveness. So why aren't these metrics studied carefully? One reason is that it's hard to know how much of a product would have sold if supply had been plentiful. The figure can be estimated using sophisticated statistical techniques, but retailers generally can't find such capabilities in commercial software, especially in the case of short-life-cycle products.

There is a way over that hurdle. We developed a method to estimate lost sales. Our procedure works in two steps. First, it calculates the underlying demand rate for a product based on the sales patterns that occurred when the product was in stock. Second, it combines the estimated demand rate with the duration of the product stockout at a particular store to derive the lost sales. To estimate demand rate and lost sales, the technique has to be modified for factors such as the variation of demand on different days and at different times within a day. In our experiments with real retail data, our technique estimated lost sales to within 2% at the store level and with higher accuracy at the chain level or for a category of products.

The benefits of tracking lost sales, and increasing inventory levels systematically to reduce those losses, can be substantial. One retailer found that sales could be improved by roughly 10% simply by increasing inventory at the stores, suggesting that lost sales—before the inventory boost—would have accounted for at least 10% of sales. At Rome-based jewelry manufacturer Bulgari, stockouts on a single item at one store had been high enough to reduce the store's revenue by 3.5%. As a result, Bulgari is seeking ways to improve its planning processes.

Accurate, Available Data

All the retailers in our study have point-of-sale (POS) systems and have used them to capture sales data electronically. But contrary to popular perception, most retailers have considerable difficulty capturing and maintaining sales data that are accurate and accessible to their employees.

First, let's consider the accuracy of the data that retailers collect. Store-level sales data are often inaccurate for several reasons. In the apparel industry, a common source of data inaccuracy arises from improper handling of returns. When a customer buys a medium sweater and then wants to exchange it for a small, the returned garment should be scanned into the register as a return, and the requested garment should be scanned in as a new purchase. In reality, the salesperson, trying not to inconvenience the customer, exchanges the medium garment for the small garment without scan-ning both items into the POS system. As a result, the inventory levels of both items are inaccurate.

In the grocery business, the sheer volume of transactions confounds the grocer's ability to maintain accurate sales and inventory information. Most consumers can recount a situation in which they bought multiple units with the same price (for example, a container of lemon yogurt and a container of vanilla yogurt, both the same brand) and the checkout clerk scanned one of these items multiple times. Clearly, this would cause the inventories of both the lemon and the vanilla yogurt to be inaccurate. One grocery chain found that sales of medium tomatoes have consistently been 25% higher than the actual shipment of medium tomatoes to their stores. Checkout clerks frequently entered into their registers the price lookup (PLU) code for "medium tomato" even if the customer was buying organic, vine-ripe, or other specialty tomatoes. "If it's red and soft, it's a medium tomato at the checkout counter," remarks the CIO at this supermarket chain. Most checkout clerks are reluctant to spend extra time to check the PLU code accurately and risk upsetting the customer and their manager, who, in many cases, is tracking the average rate at which the checkout clerks scan units.

Not all data inaccuracy is caused at the checkout register, of course. One retailer in our study found that inventory records were inaccurate for 29% of the items at a store that had been stocked but that had not yet opened for customers. The retailer traced the problem back to its distribution systems; warehouse employees often shipped the wrong item (for instance, sending small shirts instead of medium shirts, or sending one flavor of yogurt instead of another). Similarly, errors were caused when changes in vendor case-packs—the number of items shipped per box—weren't promptly entered in the retailer's merchandise replenishment system. In one instance, a vendor changed the dimensions of its case-pack from 144 units to 12 units; the merchandise replenishment system, unaware of the change, asked the warehouse to ship only one case-pack.

Many retailers don't know if their information is inaccurate because they don't track data accuracy. Other retailers track data accuracy, but the information discovered is not widely disseminated. At one apparel retailer, the merchandisers and planners had no idea their POS data were inaccurate even though the vice president of planning had, through periodic audits, concluded that the error in inventory data was close to 30% at the store level.

Some retailers have taken steps to ensure the accuracy of sales and inventory data. One interesting approach, the "zero balance walk," is practiced at office-supply superstore Staples. In this system, an employee walks through the store each day looking for SKUs that are out of stock. For each item that is out of stock, a stockout card is generated and a sticker is placed in the space reserved for the item. Other employees verify the events—sudden surges in consumer demand, computer data error, merchandise stocked in the wrong aisle, and so on—that caused the sellout. If the stockout was due to faulty data in the computer, the inventory level in the computer system is corrected. Performing the zero balance walk each day helps measure and improve data accuracy at Staples.

Now let's consider the availability of data. The retailers we surveyed varied in their ability to store and access their sales data. The median retailer in our study kept two years of sales data accessible on-line. One company kept only six weeks of data for its employees to use; at the other extreme, another company kept ten years of sales data accessible on-line.

People often wonder why it's valuable to keep a history of sales for so many years given how quickly trends change. In fact, the data contain some useful information about sales patterns that remain stable from year to year, such as seasonality, consumer reaction to a promotion, and differences in sales patterns at different stores. We have also found that the average forecast error tends to be reasonably similar from year to year, even if the products have changed almost entirely.

Forecasting product sales is much more difficult for the merchants at companies that lack sufficient on-line data. At the retailer with only six weeks' worth of on-line data, merchants referred to heavy stacks of paper copies of sales data from previous years when estimating future product sales. Given that the cost of computer storage space has fallen sharply, there's no reason for retailers not to store sales data electronically and make it easily accessible to their merchants. Those who don't either don't see how the data could be useful in their decision making or made the decision several years ago when computer storage space was extremely expensive.

Some retailers don't make even recent sales data available at the detailed level. For example, some apparel retailers track their sales according to style, color, and size (each has its own bar code) but they store only the data regarding style and color in the central computer. So a merchandiser might know how many red blouses in a certain style were sold at a particular store on a particular day but not if those units were sold in small, medium, or large. Is it any wonder that a recent survey found that one out of three consumers who enter a clothing store intending to buy something leave without buying because he or she can't find their size in stock?

Managers at these retailers claim there is little value in knowing sales by size since their vendors and distribution centers can ship only in standard size packs, which precludes customizing the size assortments by store or region. Meanwhile, it is difficult to justify changes to their transportation and warehousing systems that would let them customize their shipments, because they don't have the appropriate sales-by-size data that would tell them how to do that. It's the perfect example of the vicious cycle these retailers fall into: an inflexible supply chain justifies bad data, which justify an inflexible supply chain.

Costs, Customer Satisfaction, and Morale

We've outlined the current best practices—and the current best-case scenarios—for the four areas that are fundamental to achieving rocket science retailing. But there are other areas of improvement for retailers who seek to get closer to the grail.

Many of the issues we've touched on have dealt with metrics like forecast accuracy, stockouts, lost sales, gross margins, markdowns, and inventory carrying costs. But retailers also need to track the variables that drive those measures. For example, which products and market segments tend to have inaccurate forecasts, and how does forecast accuracy change over time? Only then will retailers have the information they need to get at the root cause of retail problems, solve them, and improve performance.

Some retailers also focus too much on the short term. The pressure to immediately improve profits can spur cost-cutting that leads to customer dissatisfaction and low employee morale. The senior managers at one retailer in our study were challenged by the board to achieve double-digit profit increases every year. Management achieved this goal by cutting costs through reducing the number of salespeople in the stores. The board was pleased with the short-term profit growth, but the reduced head-count pretty quickly created lower customer satisfaction, and employees were unhappy.

To prevent this kind of problem, retailers need to visibly and accurately track customer satisfaction and employee morale. At least one retailer in our study has engaged an outside audit firm to measure those factors, and the company is even considering reporting the results in its annual reports. That approach makes sense; without hard numbers on customer satisfaction and employee morale, those factors would take a backseat to cost reduction. In the long run the retailer would be worse off.

Marriage of Art and Science

It's useful to consider the long-standing conflict between left-brainers, the technical types who either produce or rely on information supplied through technology, and right-brainers, those who rely more on intuition. The core of rocket science retailing, as we've said, involves a marriage of the two. And many retail executives do acknowledge the need for blending left- and right-brain capabilities, particularly in planning.

Consistent with this view, their organizations have a left-brained planning organization to complement the traditionally right-brained buying or merchandising organizations. The planner typically looks at sales data—

in the absence of software systems—to determine stocking quantities at the store and SKU levels. The buyer tries to look beyond numbers and history and focuses on right-brain tasks such as identifying changing patterns in consumer demand and developing new products.

The division of skills and responsibilities between buying and planning appears to work well at most retailers. But in other areas, there is vast room for improvement; a good example is the relationship between the management information systems group, which maintains computer systems at the company, and other departments such as merchandising. One retail CEO reports "The only time [the MIS managers] communicate with me is when they ask me for a $30 million write-off on some previous project that now has to be abandoned." Another CEO chastised us for not appreciating the MIS-merchandising divide: "You guys don't get it, the merchandising-MIS relationship is broken."

Most MIS specialists aren't experts in products or merchandising. They are experts in information technologies such as database management and computer networks. Prior to joining the retailer, they may have worked at nonretail companies. Consequently, they don't always understand the needs of the merchandising organization. In many cases, even the language is substantially different between the two groups. One MIS group at a leading retailer found, much to its surprise, that when merchants in the company say "always," as in "I always follow this procedure," they mean 75% of the time. This shocked the literal-minded MIS group for whom "always" means 100%. It is not clear how the relationship between MIS and merchandising will evolve. But we don't see how merchandising can become scientific without the two factions understanding each other.

The Systems at the Core

If rocket science retailing is ever to happen across the industry, retailers must pay more attention to the logic that is embedded in their planning systems.

Most retailers, for example, realize that inventory levels should be reduced toward the end of a product's life cycle and that forecasts should be updated based on early sales data after adjusting for product availability and price fluctuations. But most inventory-planning software is designed for products that have long life cycles and is thus inappropriate for products that have an economic life of just a few months.

Consider, for example, a catalog retailer that recently bought a new software package for planning inventories of short-life-cycle products. The company was advised to set the system's parameters to stock four weeks' worth of projected demand for each SKU. For these products, however, sales usually peaked in the first week and then declined exponentially. This meant that the four-week supply ordered by the system was based on inflated sales. It was inevitably too much inventory and often generated obsolete goods at the end of the products' life cycles.

What's more, most inventory planning systems typically require two or three years of demand history on which to model forecasting and stocking parameters. This is a problem for the many products whose life cycles are measured in months. Some software vendors are starting to address this problem, and we're confident an appropriate system will be developed soon.

Rocket science retailing will require the development and use of decision support tools. In the past, many retailers that have attempted to develop such systems in-house or purchase them from third-party vendors have been disappointed; the systems did not use the appropriate mathematical techniques and hence produced poor results. The mathematical techniques underlying such decision-support systems are not straightforward for a number of reasons.

Consider a task as simple as using early sales data to guide replenishment; see what's selling well and get more of it if you can. But implementing this concept requires careful attention to detail. For example, it's important to know not just how much has sold of a particular product but the conditions under which it sold, including price and inventory availability. This point is well illustrated by one retailer that had developed a replenishment model based on early sales data. The model showed that a product in one style and color was selling almost twice as well as had been originally forecast. Based on this, a large replenishment order was placed. The vice president of merchandising who had placed the order was dismayed to see sales in the next three weeks fall to 60% of what the model had predicted. She was convinced that the model was flawed. But careful examination revealed that sales were slow because a delivery of the product that had been expected at the time the order was placed, and that had been assumed by the model, was delayed by three weeks. Hence, stores were stocking out of many sizes. Once the fresh product arrived, sales rebounded to the level predicted by the model. The underlying principle is simple—you can't sell it if you don't have it in inventory. But retailers often overlook this principle when they interpret sales data.

Nature abhors a vacuum, and the retailing situation today is an economic vacuum that cannot persist.

Retailers can't continue to suffer growing markdown losses yet disappoint a significant portion of their customers who can't find what they want. They can't continue to ignore billions of bytes of unused sales history that could help solve these problems. Somehow this vacuum will be filled.

Every decade sees a retailer that innovates so powerfully that it rewrites the rules for other retailers and for all companies in the retail supply chain. In the 1980s, it was Wal-Mart. In the 1990s, it was Amazon.com. We believe the next retail innovator will be the one that best combines access to consumer transaction data with the ability to turn that information into action.

It Happened on Wall Street

TO THOSE IMMERSED in the day-to-day operations of a retail organization, the movement toward rocket science retailing may seem overwhelming and the challenges insurmountable. But consider a similar movement on Wall Street in the late 1970s, when several ingredients came together to transform the act of investing from an art to a science.

The first ingredient was information technology that had the power to capture, store, and analyze trade data, even to the point of programmed trading in which computers traded against other computers to exploit any arbitrage opportunities that might remain open for just a few seconds. The second ingredient was new models and concepts from academia that provided a framework for analyzing all these data. And third was a new breed of Wall Street employee, who left behind a career in science and engineering to man the burgeoning science of optimized investing. Today these same ingredients are poised to transform retailing.

It may seem like a stretch to draw a parallel between a retailer and a Wall Street investment firm, but consider that both must analyze transaction data—be they stock trades or product sales—to predict the next high-flying stock or hot product. (If you think predicting the performance of stocks is fundamentally different from predicting the sales of fashion products, ask yourself whether the lofty valuation of Internet stocks has been any less a fad than consumers' infatuation with Pokemon toys.) Both must invest resources—either stocks or product inventory—in the face of risk and uncertainty. And both need to react quickly to signals from the marketplace.

These elements—accurate, available data; forecasting; risk-based inventory planning; and supply-chain speed—are the foundation of rocket science retailing.

Research Methods

OUR FORMAL RESEARCH on rocket science retailing began after discussions with retailers that had collected large amounts of consumer and sales data but were struggling to use them effectively. We decided to launch a study to document current merchandising and supply-chain practices among retailers. We felt that once we understood the retailers' supply chains well, we could identify ways in which they could be improved.

Our vision of scientific or rocket-science retailing was shared by the Sloan Foundation, a large number of retailers that supported the study, and numerous students and academics at various schools who contributed substantially to the project. For our survey, we selected mostly retailers of innovative, short-life-cycle products such as fashion apparel, shoes, toys, jewelry, books, music, entertainment software, consumer electronics, and PCs. We thought the unpredictable demand of these products would make them the hardest cases for retailers. We interacted with the retailers through site visits, written surveys, and annual conferences to understand their processes for forecasting and managing supply. The following retailers participated.

Apparel and Footwear–David's Bridal, Footstar, Gap, G. H. Bass, Maurice's, Nine West, the Limited, World Company, and Zara.

Consumer Electronics and PCs–CompUSA, Office Depot, Radio Shack, Staples, the Good Guys, and Tweeter etc.

Books, CDs, Jewelry, Toys, Theme Stores–Borders Group, Bulgari, the Disney Store, Tiffany & Company, TransWorld, Warner Brothers, and Zany Brainy.

Other Product Categories and Multiple Product Categories–Ahold, Christmas Tree Shops, CVS, Federated Group, HE Butt Grocery Company, Iceland Frozen Foods, JC Penney, Marks & Spencer, QVC, and Sears.

Originally published in July–August 2000
Reprint R00404

Welcome to the New World of Merchandising

SCOTT C. FRIEND AND
PATRICIA H. WALKER

Executive Summary

RETAILING IS AND ALWAYS has been an inefficient business. Retailers, particularly those that operate large chains, have to predict the desires of fickle consumers, buy and allocate complex sets of merchandise, set the right prices, and offer the right promotions for each individual item. Inevitably, there are gaps between supply and demand, leaving stores holding too much of what customers don't want and too little of what they do.

Now, however, a new set of software tools promises to revolutionize the entire merchandising chain. These merchandising optimization systems, as they're called, determine the right quantity, allocation, and price of items to maximize retailers' returns. By applying sophisticated data-processing techniques to existing inventory and sales data, they accurately model future patterns of supply and demand at the item and store level. In other words, they turn the art of merchandising into a science.

Early users of the new software, such as Gymboree and J.C. Penney, are already reporting promising gains in gross margins in the range of 5% to 10%. Retailers are also seeing significant increases in efficiency: At one chain, for instance, planners' productivity rose 20%. Equally important, retailers are showing improvements in customer satisfaction, as shoppers become more likely to find desired merchandise in stock at fair prices.

This article provides retailers with a guide to merchandising optimization systems, explaining how they work and how they change processes at each step of the merchandising chain.

D ON'T LET WAL-MART FOOL YOU. Retailing is and has always been an inefficient business. Retailers, particularly those that operate large chains, have to predict the desires of fickle customers, buy and allocate complex sets of merchandise, set the right prices, and offer the right promotions for each individual item. Inevitably, there are gaps, often wide ones, between supply and demand, which leave stores holding too much of what customers don't want and too little of what they do.

As product life cycles have collapsed and the mass market has fragmented, merchandising decisions have become even more complex, and the penalties for errors even steeper. Despite spending billions of dollars on point-of-sale scanners and other new computer and communication systems, retailers continue to pay high costs for their inability to get the right goods to the right places at the right prices at the right times. It is estimated that 8% of the items customers come to buy are out of stock, and that a third of all goods are sold at marked-down prices.

K-Mart alone wrote off $400 million in excess inventory in the first quarter of 2001, contributing to a 40% decline in net income. Not all retailers' problems are so extreme, but they still represent a constant drain on the bottom line, especially for those that sell merchandise with a short shelf life—whether Christmas cards, computers, or apparel.

Now, however, there may be hope for a solution. A sophisticated new set of software tools has emerged, which promises to revolutionize the entire merchandising chain—from buying to stocking to pricing. These merchandising optimization systems, as they're called, determine the right quantity, placement, and price of items to maximize retailers' returns. By applying sophisticated data-processing techniques to existing inventory and sales data, they accurately model future patterns of supply and demand at the item and store level. In other words, they turn the art of merchandising into a science.

Early users of the new software—Gymboree, J. C. Penney, KB Toys, and ShopKo, among others—are already reporting promising results, with gains in gross margins in the range of 5% to 15%. Retailers are also seeing significant increases in process efficiency. Planners at one chain, for instance, experienced a 20% gain in productivity. Equally important, retailers are showing improvements in customer satisfaction, as shoppers become more likely to find desired merchandise in stock at fair prices.

In this article, we will provide retailers—as well as wholesalers and consumer goods companies—with a guide to merchandising optimization systems. We will explain how they work and how they change processes at each step of the merchandising chain.

How It Works

The use of optimization software is nothing new in business. Yield-management applications have already brought precision pricing and capacity management to the airline and hotel industries. But until recently, merchandising optimization has been beyond the capabilities of retailers. The problem, ironically, wasn't a lack of data—it was an overabundance of data. The computing power needed to analyze the information retailers collect from hundreds of stores, thousands of products, and millions of transactions was just too expensive.

That's now changing. The continuing plunge in the price of computing cycles is bringing sophisticated optimization applications to the corporate server and desktop. Typically, these applications sit on top of and draw data from the retailer's existing management systems, such as Retek, JDA, and SAP. They apply complex algorithms to the data to model demand at the level of individual stores and individual stock-keeping units (SKUs). And because the applications are usually browser-based, everyone—from the CEO to a store manager—can easily tap into the analyses.

Retailing optimization systems vary in both size and focus: Applications can be implemented either as individual modules for specific processes or as a complete suite for the entire merchandising continuum. And the price varies accordingly. Designing, building, and deploying a system can cost anywhere between $250,000 and $5 million. Despite the high price tag, many retailers are ready and willing to embrace these new technologies. In fact, according to *InformationWeek,* out of 24 industries, specialty and general merchandise retailers spent the greatest percentage of their information technology budgets on new technology last year.

The value of merchandising optimization applications lies in their ability, first, to provide far more accurate demand forecasts and, second, to support better decisions at each step of the merchandising chain.

BETTER DEMAND FORECASTS

Traditionally, retailers have relied on last year's sales to determine this year's forecast. But that approach evaluates only what the retailer sold, not what it could have sold had the inventory been available. Clearly, information on potential sales is much more valuable, and that's what optimization software can help uncover. Through a comprehensive analysis of historical data, the software measures consumers' response to the merchandise and to each key driver of demand, such as price, inventory levels, promotions, or seasonality. This causal analysis is performed at the lowest level for which sufficient data exist. And when there's not enough information, merchandising optimization systems use clustering techniques to find other items and locations with similar demand patterns and extrapolate sales patterns from them.

It's easy to see why causal demand forecasts are so much more accurate than traditional ones. By understanding the relationship between sales and demand drivers, retailers can understand not just what results were achieved, but why. From that, they can then develop new projections by recombining the demand drivers in any number of ways.

Merchandising optimization systems are able to handle complex forecasting because they use nonlinear analytical techniques, which more closely mirror what happens in the real world. Traditional linear models can describe only one-to-one relationships between two variables—say, price and demand—with everything else held constant. For instance, a linear model would describe the relationship between a price cut on a sweater and its unit sales as a straight line: A 5% cut creates a 2% sales increase, a 10% cut creates a 4% increase, and so on. But a nonlinear model shows the price-demand relationship as a curved line. So for the same sweater, a nonlinear model might predict the following: A 5% price break creates a 2% increase, a 10% cut creates a 4% increase, but at 15%, the impact jumps to a 10% increase, and things really get going at 20%, when demand surges by 25%. Because this nonlinear approach is more consistent with actual sales performance, it results in more precise forecasts.

Nonlinear models are also better at handling the complex correlation of multiple variables. Imagine selling the same sweater two weeks before Christmas during a particularly harsh winter. The linear model still predicts that a price cut of 10% would increase sales by 4%. The nonlinear model, however, understands that customer reaction to a price cut is also a function of the time of year, so it predicts a 10% jump in sales from the same price cut that normally generates a 4% increase.

BETTER DECISIONS

Once the demand forecast has been established, the software evaluates a range of possible actions—such as cutting an item's price by 2% or putting seasonal merchandise onto store shelves earlier—and recommends the best course of action. Using sophisticated optimization mathematics, the "decision optimization engine," as this element of the software is called, analyzes the effects of adjustments to the demand drivers that the retailer controls—such as timing and pricing—on margins and other results. To put it another way, the software simulates all likely sales scenarios, evaluates the outcomes, and selects the action that produces the best results.

In recommending actions, the software takes into account all the other merchandising activities taking place. If a hardware chain, for example, holds an annual July 4th sale that cuts prices by 20%, the software wouldn't evaluate the impact of cutting a product's price by 10% that week.

The optimization engine not only works with the retailer's existing business rules—such as, "Every price must end in 99 cents,"—but also identifies what a retailer stands to gain by relaxing a specific business rule. Let's say, for example, that a retailer decides to make February 15 the transition date between winter and spring merchandise. The software could run analyses to determine that March 1 is, in fact, the optimal time to clear wool sweaters and begin selling lightweight cotton ones.

A caveat: Although objective analysis of sales data is crucial, don't overlook the role of a merchant's intuition. While mathematics is at the heart of optimization solutions, forecasts must reflect trends that aren't evident in historical data. That's particularly true with fashion merchandise. For example, only an experienced buyer could have predicted that capri pants would be hot in 1999 or that leather pants would be the rage in 2000. Such rapidly changing trends highlight the need to use common sense when analyzing the software's forecasts.

Streamlined Merchandising

Now let's look at how merchandising optimization software changes retailers' processes at each step of the merchandising chain: from planning, buying, and allocating to replenishing, pricing, and promoting. (See the exhibit "Optimizing the Merchandising Chain.")

As we've explained, merchandising optimization applications transform the planning and buying stages by creating highly accurate forecasts. Consider, for example, how the software helps a retailer plan for a summer item like shorts. In the preseason—typically at least six months before the selling season—the system determines the demand based on last year's sales of similar shorts. To determine store-level sales, it takes into account the impact of previous stockouts as well as any planned promotions or price changes for the coming season.

In the allocation stage, the software uses the latest data to identify the best way to distribute stock to each store. For instance, recent sales trends, such as a new competitor affecting sales at one store, would prompt the software to adjust its original forecast and reallocate items. It can also project which sizes will be sold in various locations. A store in Boston, for example, may sell a higher percentage of denim shorts in the smaller sizes, while a Milwaukee store may sell a higher percentage in the larger sizes. An analysis by the optimization software will recommend how many shorts to buy and in what sizes for the entire chain. (For more details, see the sidebar "Getting the Right Sizes to the Right Stores" at the end of this article.)

After the season begins, the merchandising optimization application recommends replenishment strategies

Optimizing the Merchandising Chain

Because merchandising optimization software provides recommendations based on a thorough analysis of continually updated data, it improvises every step in the retail chain. It produces more accurate forecasts, better inventory management, increased sales, and ultimately, higher gross margins.

	Planning	Buying	Allocation	Replenishment	Pricing	Promotion
Traditional approach	Bases projections on simple analysis of history and the planner's interpretation of current events	Bases decisions on simple analysis of historical sales of similar items Often develops plan at an aggregate level and spreads it to the item level	Spreads inventory to stores based on historical sales Broadly applies general rules across merchandise categories and requires subjective judgments	Uses simple algorithms that can't adjust for the latest selling patterns	Applies static rules developed from average merchandise behavior to all items	Bases decisions on last year's promotions and last year's gross sales outcomes
Optimization software approach	Assesses relative risks of investment decisions and identifies the best allocation of inventory investment	Facilitates item-and store-level planning with bottom-up and top-down analysis Calculates true demand based on what would have sold in the past if the inventory had been available	Uses store-level forecasts to precisely match inventory requirements with local demand	Generates replenishment recommendations based on in-season forecasts that use current sales and inventory data	Evaluates the demand for unique items, compares the effects of various pricing actions, and recommends the best actions	Evaluates the best items based on current sales trends and calculates incremental sales and margins for both the promoted item and its market basket

by evaluating actual sales data and readjusting forecasts for specific items. The software then makes replenishment recommendations by matching the remaining supply to the most up-to-date demand forecasts. That lets buyers place new orders or cancel existing orders based on actual sales. In addition, the software uses data on sales trends and inventory levels to help the managers make day-to-day decisions on pricing and promotions. Thus the software's recommendations provide the basis for a more rational approach to discounts and markdowns.

Making the Most of Markdowns

In fact, markdown management is where optimization software has had the greatest impact so far. Retailers use markdowns as a way to drive sales and clear excess inventory as the season progresses. But determining the optimal timing and depth of markdowns is difficult work. Aggressive markdowns (too deep, too soon) may clear inventory, but they may also unnecessarily reduce margins. By contrast, retailers who make overly conservative markdowns (too little, too late) may be stuck with excess inventory, forcing them to either make more drastic price cuts or liquidate the product at a loss.

Retailers have traditionally created static rules to tackle this problem. One retailer, for instance, flags markdown candidates when their weekly sell-through percentages fall below a certain value. Another retailer cuts prices based on shelf time—marking products down by 20% after eight weeks, then by 30% after 12 weeks, and finally by 50% after 16 weeks.

Such a rules-based approach, however, is limited in several ways. First, it assumes that all the items within a category exhibit the same, consistent behavior. So it treats a cashmere sweater the same way it treats a wool one. Second, a rules-based approach follows a fixed schedule; it's not sophisticated enough to determine how shifts in sales trends or other factors such as promotions or holidays will affect demand. And third, this approach fails to take gross margin into consideration; its only goal is to clear inventory.

Instead of relying on rules developed from averages, a retailer can benefit significantly from merchandising optimization software. It considers a range of actions for each individual item and recommends those actions that will produce the best outcome in terms of pricing and timing. The system does more than just clear inventory—it maximizes gross margin dollars by considering merchandising constraints, business goals, and in-season behavior.

Let's take a closer look at the type of analysis the software runs through to determine the best course of action. (See the exhibit "A Comparison of Markdown Scenarios.") The application analyzes thousands of different pricing and timing scenarios for markdowns. For each scenario explored, the system produces a demand forecast and calculates the expected gross margin dollars, comparing the probable outcomes of each one. Then it selects the option that will result in the highest margin.

To put that information into context, imagine that you run a national retail chain, and you need to decide how to price a product with a short shelf life—in this case, a men's winter parka. Suppose the parka was introduced in the last week in September and is scheduled to be off the selling floor by the end of March. The initial retail price is $90, the inventory is delivered all at once,

A Comparison of Markdown Scenarios

Merchandising optimization software analyzes thousands of markdown scenarios for every item in a retailer's inventory—a process that's far too complicated and time-consuming for managers to do on their own. In this example, the software compares possible markdown schedules for a parka and, based on projections of demand, highlights the sequence of price cuts that will generate the highest gross margin.

Week:	9	10	11	12	13	14	15	16	17	18	19	20	21	22	23	Expected Gross Margin
Scenario																
1834							$44.99									$73,838
1835							$54.99									$63,603
1836						$54.99										$71,360
1837					$64.99										$59.99	$79,161
1838					$59.99							$54.99				$88,823
1839				$59.99												$98,178
1840				$59.99										$54.99		$98,362
1841				$59.99									$54.99			$98,424
1842				$59.99								$54.99				$98,504
1843			$69.99								$54.99					$90,655
1844			$64.99													$98,255
1845		$64.99					$54.99									$103,654
1846		$71.99													$59.99	$89,278
1847		$64.99														$101,288
1848	$69.99				$59.99			$49.99								$105,190
1849	$71.99														$53.99	$94,754
1850	$69.99											$59.99				$99,032

and no replenishment is scheduled—which isn't unusual for merchandise with short life cycles. To simplify the example, assume that the parka has no salvage value at the end of its life cycle and that there are no disposal costs.

If you were to adopt a typical rules-based approach, you'd schedule incremental markdowns at predetermined lengths of time, in accordance with the sales forecast that was established before the beginning of the season. As shown in the exhibit "The Science of Markdowns," you would cut the parka's price by 20% after six weeks, by 30% in another five weeks, and finally by 50% after four more weeks. Using that system of planned discounts, you could expect to realize a gross margin of $98,000.

But if you had allowed your optimization software to generate a markdown schedule, you could have made a gross margin of $105,000. Why is the optimization software schedule so much more profitable? First, the application constantly refines its pricing forecasts based on actual sales throughout the season. In this example, for instance, the software recognizes that in early November, the parka's sales patterns are better than expected, so it delays taking the price reduction that the rules-based approach demands. Each week, as fresh sales data become available, it readjusts the forecasts to include the latest information. It computes literally thousands of scenarios for each item—a process that is too complicated and time-consuming for retailers to do on their own. Ultimately, the system recommends cutting your price from $90 to $69.99 in the ninth week, to $59.99 in the 13th week, and to $49.99 in the 16th week—timing the markdowns to take effect just before the Thanksgiving and Christmas rushes. In this example, you could have made 7% more on your sales of men's parkas using optimization software than by following a rules-based approach. The cumulative effect of gains like that across your entire inventory would significantly boost your bottom line.

Are You Ready?

No doubt, a merchandising optimization system can produce extraordinary results. But before you decide to implement one at your business, you'd be wise to ask the following questions:

Do you have the necessary information technology capabilities? Merchandising optimization systems

---

The Science of Markdowns

The benefits of using optimization software are perhaps best illustrated in the area of markdown management. This chart shows that one retailer could increase its gross margin on a parka by 7% by relying on optimization software. Because the software continually refines its forecasts based on current sales patterns, store managers know exactly when to lower prices, and by how much, to generate the most profit.

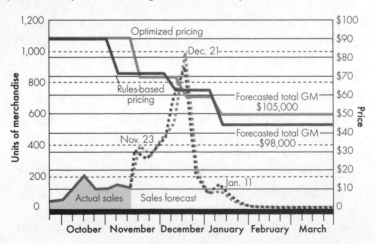

use data from your existing point-of-sale and inventory management systems to make forecasts and recommendations. For the system to perform effectively, those data must be captured accurately. Moreover, if you have a well-organized data mart or warehouse, it will be easier for the system to locate and analyze the proper data.

Can the software be configured for your business? No matter how powerful a system is, it is useless unless it works in your particular environment. After all, what good is a recommendation to promote an item at 17.23% off if your pricing package supports discounts of only 10%, 20%, and so on? Before you implement the optimization software, be sure it can be configured to meet your operational constraints.

Does the software support your merchandising strategy? Before you invest in a new merchandising optimization system, be sure it can support your current strategy. If you're a bricks-and-mortar retailer with an outlet channel, for example, you'll need a system that can pinpoint when to clear the merchandise from your regular store and move it into the outlet. Additionally, you should be prepared to revisit your existing strategies in light of your new capabilities. A retailer that has always assumed that pricing decisions should be made at the chain level, for instance, would be well advised to reevaluate that process: Perhaps it makes more sense to set prices at the regional or even the local-market level.

Are you willing to reassess your internal processes? Optimization software automates many manual processes, eliminating the need for temporary "work arounds" to address system inadequacies. But to reap the benefits of all the workflow enhancements of the software, you may need to reassess some of your internal processes. For example, you'll need to provide training and coaching to employees to ensure that the system's recommendations are being followed. And you must constantly measure internal compliance as well as the actual results of the software. One of the toughest challenges might be getting managers—used to relying on their instincts—to trust the system's forecasts and numbers.

THE RETAILING BUSINESS IS not getting any easier: New distribution channels and novel formats are nibbling at gross margins, the life cycles of products are shortening, fickle customers are becoming more demanding, and erratic changes in demand are forcing retailers to make decisions faster than ever before. Worse, consolidation is creating ever-larger chains, which means retailers must manage hundreds of stores—stocking thousands of products and making thousands of pricing and inventory decisions for each item at each store each week.

It's no wonder that retailers are clamoring for better tools. By leveraging the latest in mathematical modeling techniques and the power of information technology, merchandising optimization software helps retailers efficiently and profitably manage their business. We don't claim that the software is a cure-all: Retail operations are too complex and the difficulty of ensuring data integrity too severe to promise that. However, given the industry's myriad challenges, the time is right for a technology that brings control to what was risky, rigor to what was intuitive, and science to what was guesswork.

Getting the Right Sizes to the Right Stores

ALLOCATING THE RIGHT MIX OF merchandise to each store is one of the biggest challenges faced by retailers. That's particularly true of clothing merchants. They struggle to match the right mix of sizes to store-level demand, which usually results in lost sales in underallocated sizes as well as heavier markdowns in overallocated sizes. Merchandising optimization software uses historical sales data to understand and respond to real demand by size and then determines the best allocation.

Retailers have always relied on last year's sales history to determine this year's size assortment. The question, however, should not be, "What has historically sold?" but rather, "What would have sold had the right sizes been available?" Past data simply cannot answer this question because of varying stockout times across sizes, followed by subsequent markdowns on the remaining sizes. To get a more accurate measure of demand, retailers must first unearth the true demand for each size by scrubbing these biases from the historical data. A retailer that doesn't perform this critical step will be doomed to repeat past mistakes.

The graph shows the purchase-size profile for women's pants based on historical sales for a retailer that distributes merchandise according to a single size profile for the entire chain. Juxtaposed against the traditional profile are the optimal size profiles for women's pants in Chicago and San Francisco. Clearly, allocating the same distribution of sizes to the Chicago and San Francisco stores would be a mistake: The San Francisco stores would sell out of smaller sizes early and have too many larger sizes. The Chicago stores would have the opposite problem.

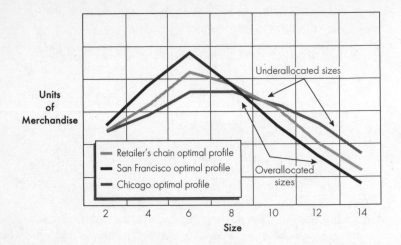

Merchandising optimization software, by contrast, can identify a specific size profile for each store and then match supply to local demand. Retailers, however, may not want to implement decisions at this level because of the associated costs. (The additional logistical and operational costs increase with the number of size profiles, and the total costs depend on the retailers' system capabilities, store layout capabilities, and the vendors' ability to pack and ship multiple size combinations.) If that's the case, the application can determine the optimal number of size profiles and create store clusters with similar size profiles.

Do You Need It?

MERCHANDISING OPTIMIZATION solutions are most appropriate for retailers that:

- *Sell products that have a short shelf life or have uncertain demand.* Fads in clothes and music, for instance, shift rapidly, while seasonal items like air conditioners have sharp demand spikes. Products characterized by rapid innovation, like computer systems, also have short life cycles. And even relatively stable products like toothpaste and office supplies can have highly uncertain demand during promotions. Optimization software can help merchants of products like these sell the most inventory at the highest margin.

- *Operate complex processes with many decision-making points.* If you operate a chain that has multiple stores and sells hundreds of items, you can't create demand forecasts with the accuracy that optimization systems can.

- *Cannot recover easily from wrong decisions.* Imagine, for instance, a retailer that sends too many Christmas decorations to one store. The stock will be of little value after December 25. A merchandising optimization application would have helped the manager make a more informed decision before the shipment was sent.

Originally published in November 2001
Reprint R0110K

Mind Your Pricing Cues

ERIC ANDERSON AND DUNCAN SIMESTER

Executive Summary

FOR MOST OF THE ITEMS they buy, consumers don't
have an accurate sense of what the price should be. Ask
them to guess how much a four-pack of 35-mm film costs,
and you'll get a variety of wrong answers: Most people
will underestimate; many will only shrug.

Research shows that consumers' knowledge of the
market is so far from perfect that it hardly deserves to be
called knowledge at all. Yet people happily buy film and
other products every day. Is this because they don't care
what kind of deal they're getting? No. Remarkably, it's
because they rely on retailers to tell them whether they're
getting a good price. In subtle and not-so-subtle ways,
retailers send signals to customers, telling them whether a
given price is relatively high or low.

In this article, the authors review several common pricing cues retailers use—"sale" signs, prices that end in 9,

signpost items, and price-matching guarantees. They also offer some surprising facts about how—and how well— those cues work. For instance, the authors' tests with several mail-order catalogs reveal that including the word "sale" beside a price can increase demand by more than 50%. The practice of using a 9 at the end of a price to denote a bargain is so common, you'd think customers would be numb to it. Yet in a study the authors did involving a women's clothing catalog, they increased demand by a third just by changing the price of a dress from $34 to $39.

Pricing cues are powerful tools for guiding customers' purchasing decisions, but they must be applied judiciously. Used inappropriately, the cues may breach customers' trust, reduce brand equity, and give rise to lawsuits.

I F YOU AREN'T SURE, you're not alone: For most of the items they buy, consumers don't have an accurate sense of what the price should be. Consider the findings of a study led by Florida International University professor Peter R. Dickson and University of Florida professor Alan G. Sawyer in which researchers with clipboards stood in supermarket aisles pretending to be stock takers. Just as a shopper would place an item in a cart, a researcher would ask him or her the price. Less than half the customers gave an accurate answer. Most underestimated the price of the product, and more than 20% did not even venture a guess; they simply had no idea of the true price.

This will hardly come as a surprise to fans of *The Price Is Right*. This game show, a mainstay of CBS's daytime programming since 1972, features contestants in a variety of situations in which they must guess the price of packaged goods, appliances, cars, and other retail products. The inaccuracy of the guesses is legendary, with contestants often choosing prices that are off by more than 50%. It turns out this is reality TV at its most real. Consumers' knowledge of the market is so far from perfect that it hardly deserves to be called knowledge at all.

One would expect this information gap to be a major stumbling block for customers. A woman trying to decide whether to buy a blouse, for example, has several options: Buy the blouse, find a less expensive blouse elsewhere on the racks, visit a competing store to compare prices, or delay the purchase in the hopes that the blouse will be discounted. An informed buying decision requires more than just taking note of a price tag. Customers also need to know the prices of other items, the prices in other stores, and what prices might be in the future.

Yet people happily buy blouses every day. Is this because they don't care what kind of deal they're getting? Have they given up all hope of comparison shopping? No. Remarkably, it's because they rely on the retailer to tell them if they're getting a good price. In subtle and not-so-subtle ways, retailers send signals to customers, telling them whether a given price is relatively high or low.

In this article, we'll review the most common pricing cues retailers use, and we'll reveal some surprising facts about how—and how well—those cues work. All the cues we will discuss—things like sale signs and prices ending in 9—are common marketing techniques. If used appropriately, they can be effective tools for building trust with customers and convincing them to buy your products and services. Used inappropriately, however, these pricing cues may breach customers' trust, reduce brand equity, and give rise to lawsuits.

Sale Signs

The most straightforward of the pricing cues retailers use is the sale sign. It usually appears somewhere near the discounted item, trumpeting a bargain for customers. Our own tests with several mail-order catalogs reveal that using the word "sale" beside a price (without actually varying the price) can increase demand by more than 50%. Similar evidence has been reported in experiments conducted with university students and in retail stores.

Placing a sale sign on an item costs the retailer virtually nothing, and stores generally make no commitment to a particular level of discount when using the signs. Admittedly, retailers do not always use such signs truthfully. There have been incidents in which a store has claimed that a price has been discounted when, in fact, it hasn't—making for wonderful newspaper articles. Consultant and former Harvard Business School professor Gwen Ortmeyer, in a review of promotional pricing policies, cites a 1990 *San Francisco Chronicle* article in which a reporter priced the same sofa at several Bay Area furniture stores. The sofa was on sale for $2,170 at one store; the regular price was $2,320. And it cost $2,600—"35% off" the original price of $4,000—at another store. Last year, a research team from the *Boston Globe* undertook a four-month investigation of prices charged by Kohl's department stores, focusing on the chain's Medford, Massachusetts, location. The team concluded that the store often exaggerated its discounts by inflating its regular prices. For instance, a Little Tikes toy truck was never sold at the regular price throughout the period of the study, according to the *Globe* article.

So why do customers trust sale signs? Because they are accurate most of the time. Our interviews with store managers, and our own observations of actual prices at department and specialty stores, confirm that when an item is discounted, it almost invariably has a sale sign posted nearby. The cases where sale signs are placed on nondiscounted items are infrequent enough that the use of such signs is still valid.

And besides, customers are not that easily fooled. They learn to recognize that even a dealer of Persian rugs will eventually run out of "special holidays" and occasions to celebrate with a sale. They are quick to adjust their attitudes toward sale signs if they perceive evidence of overuse, which reduces the credibility of discount claims and makes this pricing cue far less effective.

The link between a retailer's credibility and its overuse of sale signs was the subject of a study we conducted involving purchases of frozen fruit juice at a Chicago supermarket chain. The analysis of the sales data revealed that the more sale signs used in the category, the less effective those signs were at increasing demand. Specifically, putting sale signs on more than 30% of the items diminished the effectiveness of the pricing cue. (See the exhibit "The Diminishing Return of Sale Signs.")

A similar test we conducted with a women's clothing catalog revealed that demand for an item with a sale sign went down by 62% when sale signs were also added to other items. Another study we conducted with a publisher revealed a similar falloff in catalog orders when more than 25% of the items in the catalog were on sale. Retailers face a trade-off: Placing sale signs on multiple items can increase demand for those items—but it can also reduce overall demand. Total category sales are highest when some, but not all, items in the category have sale signs. Past a certain point, use of additional sale signs will cause total category sales to fall.

Misuse of sale signs can also result in prosecution. Indeed, several department stores have been targeted by state attorneys general. The cases often involve jewelry departments, where consumers are particularly in the dark about relative quality, but have also come to include a wide range of other retail categories, including furniture and men's and women's clothing. The lawsuits generally argue that the stores have breached state legislation on unfair or deceptive pricing. Many states have

---

The Diminishing Return of Sale Signs

Our research indicates there is a point at which adding more sale signs yields fewer sales. In a Chicago supermarket's frozen fruit juice category, charted below, putting sale signs on more than 30% of the items reduced demand substantially.

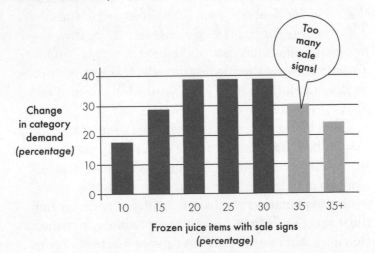

enacted legislation addressing this issue, much of it mir-
roring the Federal Trade Commission's regulations
regarding deceptive pricing. Retailers have had to pay
fines ranging from $10,000 to $200,000 and have had to
agree to desist from such practices.

Prices That End in 9

Another common pricing cue is using a 9 at the end of a
price to denote a bargain. In fact, this pricing tactic is so
common, you'd think customers would ignore it. Think
again. Response to this pricing cue is remarkable. You'd
generally expect demand for an item to go down as the
price goes up. Yet in our study involving the women's
clothing catalog, we were able to increase demand by a
third by *raising* the price of a dress from $34 to $39. By
comparison, changing the price from $34 to $44 yielded
no difference in demand. (See the exhibit "The Surprising Effect of a 9.")

This favorable effect extends beyond women's clothing catalogs; similar findings have also been reported for
groceries. Moreover, the effect is not limited to whole-
dollar figures: In their 1996 research, Rutgers University
professor Robert Schindler and then-Wharton graduate
student Thomas Kibarian randomly mailed customers of
a women's clothing catalog different versions of the catalog. One included prices that ended in 00 cents, and the
other included prices that ended in 99 cents. The professors found that customers who received the latter version were more likely to place an order. As a result, the
clothing company increased its revenue by 8%.

One explanation for this surprising outcome is that
the 9 at the end of the price acts the same way as the sale
sign does, helping customers evaluate whether they're

getting a good deal. Buyers are often more sensitive to price endings than they are to actual price changes, which raises the question: Are prices that end in 9 truly accurate as pricing cues? The answer varies. Some retailers do reserve prices that end in 9 for their discounted items. For instance, J. Crew and Ralph Lauren generally use 00-cent endings on regularly priced merchandise and 99-cent endings on discounted items. Comparisons of prices at major department stores reveal that this is common, particularly for apparel. But at some stores, prices that end in 9 are a miscue—they are used on all products regardless of whether the items are discounted.

Research also suggests that prices ending in 9 are less effective when an item already has a sale sign. This shouldn't be a surprise. The sale sign informs customers

---

The Surprising Effect of a 9

Customers react favorably when they see prices that end in 9. For instance, when a national women's clothing catalog raised the price of one of its dresses from $34 to $39, sales jumped up. But, when the price was raised from $34 to $44, there was no change in demand.

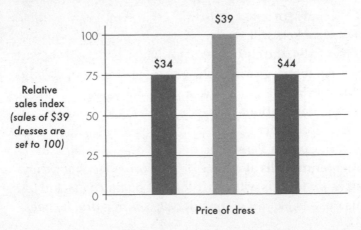

that the item is discounted, so little information is added by the price ending.

Signpost Items

For most items, customers do not have accurate price points they can recall at a moment's notice. But each of us probably knows some benchmark prices, typically on items we buy frequently. Many customers, for instance, know the price of a 12-ounce can of Coke or the cost of admission to a movie, so they can distinguish expensive and inexpensive price levels for such "signpost" items without the help of pricing cues.

Research suggests that customers use the prices of signpost items to form an overall impression of a store's prices. That impression then guides their purchase of other items for which they have less price knowledge. While very few customers know the price of baking soda (around 70 cents for 16 ounces), they do realize that if a store charges more than $1 for a can of Coke it is probably also charging a premium on its baking soda. Similarly, a customer looking to purchase a new tennis racket might first check the store's price on a can of tennis balls. If the balls are less than $2, the customer will assume the tennis rackets will also be low priced. If the balls are closer to $4, the customer will walk out of the store without any tennis gear—and the message that the bargains are elsewhere.

The implications for retailers are important, and many already act accordingly. Supermarkets often take a loss on Coke or Pepsi, and many sporting-goods stores offer tennis balls at a price below cost. (Of course, they make up for this with their sales of baking soda and tennis rackets.) If you're considering sending pricing cues through signpost items, the first question is which items to select. Three words are worth keeping in mind: *accurate, popular,* and *complementary.* That is, unlike with sale signs and prices that end in 9, the signpost item strategy is intended to be used on products for which price knowledge is accurate. Selecting popular items to serve as pricing signposts increases the likelihood that consumers' price knowledge will be accurate—and may also allow a retailer to obtain volume discounts from suppliers and preserve some margin on the sales. Both of these benefits explain why a department store is more likely to prominently advertise a basic, white T-shirt than a seasonal, floral print. And complementary items can serve as good pricing signposts. For instance, Best Buy sold *Spider-Man* DVDs at several dollars below wholesale price, on the very first weekend they were available. The retail giant lost money on every DVD sold—but its goal was to increase store traffic and generate purchases of complementary items, such as DVD players.

Signposts can be very effective, but remember that consumers are less likely to make positive inferences about a store's pricing policies and image if they can attribute the low price they're being offered to special circumstances. For example, if everyone knows there is a glut of computer memory chips, then low prices on chip-intensive products might be attributed to the market and not to the retailer's overall pricing philosophy. Phrases such as "special purchase" should be avoided. The retailer's goal should be to convey an overarching image of low prices, which then translates into sales of other items. Two retailers we studied, Golf-Joy.com and Baby's Room, include the phrase "our low regular price" in their marketing copy to create the perception that all of their prices are low. And Wal-Mart, of course, is the master of this practice.

A related issue is the magnitude of the claimed discounts. For example, a discount retailer may sell a can of tennis balls for a regular price of $1.99 and a sale price of $1.59, saving the consumer 40 cents. By contrast, a competing, higher-end retailer that matches the discount store's sale price of $1.59 may offer a regular price of $2.59, saving the consumer $1. By using the phrase "low regular price," the low-price retailer explains to consumers why its discounts may be smaller (40 cents versus $1 off) and creates the perception that all of its products are underpriced. For the higher-end competitor, the relative savings it offers to consumers ($1 versus 40 cents off) may increase sales of tennis balls but may also leave consumers thinking that the store's nonsale prices are high.

Use of signpost items to cue customers' purchases and to raise a store's pricing image creates few legal concerns. The reason for this is clear: Customers' favorable responses to this cue arise without the retailer making an explicit claim or promise to support their assumptions. While a retailer may commit itself to selling tennis balls at $2, it does not promise to offer a low price on tennis rackets. Charging low prices on the tennis balls may give the appearance of predatory pricing. But simply selling below cost is generally not sufficient to prove intent to drive competitors out of business.

Pricing Guarantees

So far, we've focused on pricing cues that consumers rely on—and that are reliable. Far less clear is the reliability of another cue, known as price matching. It's a tactic used widely in retail markets, where stores that sell, for example, electronics, hardware, and groceries promise to meet or beat any competitor's price.

Tweeter, a New England retailer of consumer electronics, takes the promise one step further: It self-enforces its price-matching policy. If a competitor advertises a lower price, Tweeter refunds the difference to any customers who paid a higher price at Tweeter in the previous 30 days. Tweeter implements the policy itself, so customers don't have to compare the competitors' prices. If a competitor advertises a lower price for a piece of audio equipment, for example, Tweeter determines which customers are entitled to a refund and sends them a check in the mail.

Do customers find these price-matching policies reassuring? There is considerable evidence that they do. For example, in a study conducted by University of Maryland marketing professors Sanjay Jain and Joydeep Srivastava, customers were presented with descriptions of a variety of stores. The researchers found that when price-matching guarantees were part of the description, customers were more confident that the store's prices were lower than its competitors'.

But is that trust justified? Do companies with price-matching policies really charge lower prices? The evidence is mixed, and, in some cases, the reverse may be true. After a large-scale study of prices at five North Carolina supermarkets, University of Houston professor James Hess and University of California at Davis professor Eitan Gerstner concluded that the effects of price-matching policies are twofold. First, they reduce the level of price dispersion in the market, so that all retailers tend to have similar prices on items that are common across stores. Second, they appear to lead to *higher* prices overall. Indeed, some pricing experts argue that price-matching policies are not really targeted at customers; rather, they represent an explicit warning to competitors: "If you cut your prices, we will, too." Even more threatening is a policy that promises to beat the price difference: "If you cut your prices, we will undercut you." This logic has led some industry observers to interpret price-matching policies as devices to reduce competition.

Closely related to price-matching policies are the most-favored-nation policies used in business-to-business relationships, under which suppliers promise customers that they will not sell to any other customers at a lower price. These policies are attractive to business customers because they can relax knowing that they are getting the best price. These policies have also been associated with higher prices. A most-favored-nation policy effectively says to your competitors: "I am committing not to cut my prices, because if I did, I would have to rebate the discount to all of my former customers."

Price-matching guarantees are effective when consumers have poor knowledge of the prices of many products in a retailer's mix. But these guarantees are certainly not for every store. For instance, they don't make sense if your prices tend to be higher than your competitors'. The British supermarket chain Tesco learned this when a small competitor, Essential Sports, discounted Nike socks to 10p a pair, undercutting Tesco by £7.90. Tesco had promised to refund twice the difference and had to refund so much money to customers that one man walked away with 12 new pairs of socks plus more than £90 in his wallet.

To avoid such exposure, some retailers impose restrictions that make the price-matching guarantee difficult to enforce. Don't try it: Customers, again, are not so easily fooled. If the terms of the deal are too onerous, they will recognize that the guarantee lacks substance. Their reaction will be the same if it proves impossible to compare prices across competing stores. (Clearly, the strategy makes no sense for retailers selling private-label or otherwise exclusive brands.) How much of the merchandise needs to be directly comparable for consumers to get a favorable impression of the company? Surprisingly little. When Tweeter introduced its highly effective automatic price-matching policy, only 6% of its transactions were actually eligible for refunds.

Interestingly, some manufacturers are making it harder for consumers to enforce price-matching policies by introducing small differences in the items they supply to different retailers. Such use of branded variants is common in the home-electronics market, where many manufacturers use different model numbers for products shipped to different retailers. The same is true in the mattress market—it is often difficult to find an identical mattress at competing retailers. If customers come to recognize and anticipate these strategies, price-matching policies will become less effective.

Antitrust concerns have been raised with regard to price-matching policies and most-favored-nation clauses. In one pending case, coffin retailer Direct Casket is suing funeral homes in New York for allegedly conspiring to implement price-matching policies. The defendants in this case have adopted a standard defense, arguing that price-matching policies are evidence of vigorous competition rather than an attempt to thwart it. An older, but perhaps even more notorious, example involved price-matching policies introduced by General Electric and Westinghouse in 1963 in the market for electric generators. The practice lasted for many years, but ultimately the U.S. Justice Department, in the early 1980s, concluded that the policies restrained price competition and were a breach of the Sherman Antitrust Act. GE and Westinghouse submitted to a consent decree under which they agreed to abandon the business practice.

Tracking Effectiveness

To maximize the effectiveness of pricing cues, retailers should implement them systematically. Ongoing measurement should be an essential part of any retailer's use of pricing cues. In fact, measurements should begin even before a pricing cue strategy is implemented to help determine which items should receive the cues and how many should be used. Following implementation, testing should focus on monitoring the cues' effectiveness. We've found that three important concerns tend to be overlooked.

First, marketers often fail to consider the long-run impact of the cues. According to some studies, pricing policies that are designed to maximize short-run profits often lead to suboptimal profits in the long run. For example, a study we conducted with a publisher's catalog from 1999 to 2001 investigated how customers respond to price promotions. Do customers return in the future and purchase more often, or do they stock up on the promoted items and come back less frequently in subsequent months? The answer was different for first-time versus established customers. Shoppers who saw deep discounts on their first purchase returned more often and purchased more items when they came back. By contrast, established customers would stock up, returning less often and purchasing fewer items. If the publisher were to overlook these long-run effects, it would set prices too low for established patrons and too high for first-time buyers.

Second, retail marketers tend to focus more on customers' perceptions of price than on their perceptions of quality. (See the sidebar "Quality Has Its Own Cues"at the end of this article.) But companies can just as easily monitor quality perceptions by varying their use of pricing cues and by asking customers for feedback.

Finally, even when marketers have such data under their noses, they too often fail to act. They need to both disseminate what is learned and change business policies. For example, to prevent overuse of promotions, May Department Stores explicitly limits the percentage of items on sale in any one department. It's not an obvious move; one might expect that the department managers would be best positioned to determine how many sale signs to use. But a given department manager is focused on his or her own department and may not consider the impact on other departments. Using additional sale signs may increase demand within one department but harm demand elsewhere. To correct this, a corporate-wide policy limits the discretion of the department managers. Profitability depends both on maintaining an effective testing program and institutionalizing the findings.

CONSUMERS IMPLICITLY TRUST retailers' pricing cues and, in doing so, place themselves in a vulnerable position. Some retailers might be tempted to breach this trust and behave deceptively. That would be a grave mistake. In addition to legal concerns, retailers should recognize that consumers need price information, just as they need products. And they look to retailers to provide both.

Retailers must manage pricing cues in the same way that they manage quality. That is, no store or catalog interested in collecting large profits in the long run would purposely offer a defective product; similarly, no retailer interested in cultivating a long-term relationship with customers would deceive them with inaccurate pricing cues. By reliably signaling which prices are low, companies can retain customers' trust—and overcome their suspicions that they could find a better deal elsewhere.

Cue, Please

PRICING CUES LIKE SALE SIGNS and prices that end in 9 become less effective the more they are employed, so it's important to use them only where they pack the most punch. That is, use pricing cues on the items for which customers' price knowledge is poor. Consider employing cues on items when one or more of the following conditions apply:

Customers purchase infrequently. The difference in consumers' knowledge of the price of a can of Coke versus a box of baking soda can be explained by the relative infrequency with which most customers purchase baking soda.

Customers are new. Loyal customers generally have better price knowledge than new customers, so it makes sense to make heavier use of sale signs and prices that end in 9 for items targeted at newer customers. This is particularly true if your products are exclusive. If, on the other hand, competitors sell identical products, new customers may have already acquired price knowledge from them.

Product designs vary over time. Because tennis racket manufacturers tend to update their models frequently, customers who are looking to replace their old rackets will always find different models in the stores or on-line, which makes it difficult for them to compare prices from one year to the next. By contrast, the design of tennis balls rarely changes, and the price remains relatively static over time.

Prices vary seasonally. The prices of flowers, fruits, and vegetables vary when supply fluctuates. Because customers cannot directly observe these fluctuations, they cannot judge whether the price of apples is high because there is a shortage or because the store is charging a premium.

Quality or sizes vary across stores. How much should a chocolate cake cost? It all depends on the size and the quality of the cake. Because there is no such thing as a standard-size cake, and because quality is hard to determine without tasting the cake, customers may find it difficult to make price comparisons.

These criteria can help you target the right items for pricing cues. But you can also use them to distinguish among different types of customers. Those who are least informed about price levels will be the most responsive to your pricing cues, and—particularly in an on-line or direct mail setting—you can vary your use of the cues accordingly.

How do you know which customers are least informed? Again, those who are new to a category or a retailer and who purchase only occasionally tend to be most in the dark.

Of course, the most reliable way to identify which customers' price knowledge is poor (and which items they're unsure about) is simply to poll them. Play your own version of *The Price Is Right*—show a sample of customers your products, and ask them to predict the prices. Different types of customers will have different answers.

Quality Has Its Own Cues

RETAILERS MUST BALANCE their efforts to cultivate a favorable price image with their efforts to protect the company's quality image. Customers often interpret discounts as a signal of weak demand, which may raise doubts about quality.

This trade-off was illustrated in a recent study we conducted with a company that sells premium-quality gifts and jewelry. The merchant was considering offering a plan by which customers could pay for a product in installments without incurring finance charges. Evidence elsewhere suggested that offering such a plan could increase demand. To test the effectiveness of this strategy, the merchant conducted a test mailing in which a random sample of 1,000 customers received a catalog that contained the installment-billing offer, while another 1,000 customers received a version of the catalog without any such offer. The company received 13% *fewer* orders from the installment-billing version, and follow-up surveys revealed that the offer had damaged the overall quality image of the catalog. As one customer cogently put it: "People must be cutting back, or maybe they aren't as rich as [the company] thought, because suddenly everything is installment plan. It makes [the company] look tacky to have installment plans."

Sale signs may also raise concerns about quality. It is for this reason that we see few sale signs in industries where perceptions of high quality are essential. For instance, an eye surgeon in the intensely competitive market for LASIK procedures commented: "Good medicine never goes on sale."

The owner of a specialty women's clothing store in Atlanta offered a similar rationale for why she does not use sale signs to promote new items. Her customers interpret sale items as leftovers from previous seasons, or mistakes, for which demand is disappointing because the item is unfashionable.

Originally published in September 2003
Reprint R0309G

Control Your Inventory
in a World of Lean Retailing

FREDERICK H. ABERNATHY,

JOHN T. DUNLOP, JANICE H. HAMMOND,

AND DAVID WEIL

Executive Summary

AS RETAILERS ADOPT lean retailing practices, manufacturers are feeling the pinch. Retailers no longer place large seasonal orders for goods in advance—instead, they require ongoing replenishment of stock, forcing manufacturers to predict demand and then hold substantial inventories indefinitely. Manufacturers now carry the cost of inventory risk—the possibility that demand will dry up and goods will have to be sold below cost. And as product proliferation increases, customer demand becomes harder to predict.

Most manufacturers apply one inventory policy for all stock-keeping units in a product line. But the inventory demand for SKUs within the same product line can vary significantly. SKUs with high volume typically have little variation in weekly sales, while slow-selling SKUs can vary enormously in weekly sales. The greater the variation, the larger the inventory the manufacturer must hold relative to an SKU's expected weekly sales. By differentiating inventory policies at the SKU level, manufacturers can reduce inventories for the high-volume SKUs and increase them for the low-volume ones—and thereby improve the profitability of the entire line.

SKU-level differentiation can also be applied to sourcing strategies. Instead of producing all the SKUs for a product line at a single location, either offshore at low cost or close to market at higher cost, manufacturers can typically do better by going for a mixed allocation. Low-variation goods should be produced mainly offshore, while high-variation goods are best made close to markets.

MANUFACTURERS OF CONSUMER GOODS are in the hot seat these days. In the past, retailers would place large orders at the beginning of each selling season, and factories would simply produce to order. But the big chain stores are increasingly adopting lean retailing practices, so they're insisting that manufacturers fill orders to replenish retailers' stock on an ongoing basis. Because factories usually can't produce goods fast enough to meet these orders, manufacturers often hold large inventories for indefinite periods.

And the cost of holding these inventories is only growing. Consumers are demanding greater variety in products, and their preferences are getting harder to predict. As products proliferate and become more susceptible to changing whims, the risk grows that a given product line will have disappointing sales and have to be discounted. But if a manufacturer decides to go lean on inventories, it runs the risk of stockouts, lost sales, and endangered relationships with the chains.

It's a tough position, but a new approach can help manufacturers predict their inventory needs more accurately. Manufacturers tend to treat every stock-keeping unit within a product line the same way—but in fact, these SKUs often have very different levels of demand. By differentiating SKUs according to their actual demand patterns, you can reduce inventories on some SKUs and increase them on others—thereby improving your profitability for the entire line.

Differentiating SKUs can also help you rethink your sourcing strategy. Instead of producing all the SKUs for a product line at a single location, either offshore at low cost or close to market at a higher cost, you can typically do better by going for a mixed allocation. That way, you can meet the demands of retailers while controlling costs and inventory.

The Inventory Dilemma

To illustrate, let's consider the inventory problems of a hypothetical company called Jeansco. In the 1980s, this blue-jeans manufacturer offered about 1,000 different SKUs—a dozen styles of jeans spread across a few dozen sizes, with total annual sales of 20 million pairs. Each season, Jeansco built up its inventories in preparation for big shipments to retailers. The inventories were enormous just before the shipment date, but the risk was small because all of those jeans matched actual orders retailers had submitted several months before. Inventory, in fact, was just a means of spreading out the demand so factories could achieve a steady, efficient flow of output. For Jeansco, the only cost of inventory lay in the working capital tied up there and in the minor expense of the warehouse. The retailers bore the major cost of inventory—the risk that sales would prove disappointing and the jeans would have to be marked down below cost.

Then in the 1990s, partly to minimize this risk, most of Jeansco's retailers began to adopt lean retailing practices. They shifted most of their ongoing inventories—and risk—back to Jeansco by keeping on-site inventories low and placing weekly replenishment orders. Since the lead time for manufacturing jeans was several weeks, Jeansco could no longer make to order; it now had to predict the weekly demand for jeans and set production schedules accordingly. And even if Jeansco got the average weekly demand right, it also had to take into account those weeks with unusually large orders. To ensure that it could fill those orders and keep its retail customers happy, Jeansco had to estimate the weekly variability in demand and hold a safety stock of finished goods in inventory.

That's difficult enough, but product proliferation only made things worse. In the 1980s, most of Jeansco's 1,000 SKUs garnered fairly high sales. Big volume tended to smooth out the inevitable peaks and valleys of demand. That meant the composite weekly demand was fairly predictable and variability wasn't so great, so the safety stock held in inventories was relatively small.

Today, Jeansco manufactures far more styles and sizes than before—it now offers 30,000 SKUs. And while total annual sales have risen to 90 million pairs, average sales per SKU have fallen from 20,000 units to just 3,000—or approximately 60 sales per SKU a week, much lower than the 1980 average of 400. And that's just an

average. Popular SKUs register hundreds or even thousands of sales per week, but less popular, highly differentiated items may sell only ten across all retail stores. The
smaller the volume of sales for any individual SKU, the
more those sales tend to vary each week because there is
so much less demand to pool together. That means
Jeansco has to stock a lot more than ten pairs of those
slow-selling jeans to meet sudden upsurges in demand—
or risk angering important customers with stockouts.
For the same overall level of sales, the company now has
to hold a much bigger overall inventory.

And what happens to Jeansco when certain styles go
out of fashion? Retailers stop placing replenishment
orders and all those multiple SKUs in inventory have to
go to discounters, eating away most of Jeansco's profit.
To take an example from the real world, look at what
happened recently when demand for athletic shoes suddenly dropped as consumers moved to brown shoes.
Nike and its competitors had to take a huge financial hit
to dispose of their bulging inventories. In the absence of
lean retailing and product proliferation, those losses
would have been far smaller.

Product proliferation has transformed retail categories far beyond apparel, from office products to pasta.
And the trend isn't going away, despite the fervent
wishes of many manufacturers, who complain about
erratic orders from retailers. We recently met with an
executive who told us business was good, except that
low-volume items were causing him fits because retailers
kept asking for greatly varying quantities. "If I could just
smooth out that demand," he said, "I'd be fine." Even
now, most manufacturers don't think this is their problem to address. Because inventory costs are often hard to

measure, losses like Nike's are usually dismissed as special, unpredictable charges. But the long-term negative effect on profit can be substantial.

Rethinking Your Product Categories

Manufacturers generally classify products in terms of broad product lines, developing a single marketing strategy and production plan for each line. That makes sense for marketing, but it's a mistake for production. Different SKUs within a product line can have very different inventory needs.

Take, for example, a large American manufacturer of men's blazers. As part of our research into lean retailing, we tracked the demand for different sizes of a blue blazer. Far from a trendy fashion item, the blue blazer is a staple of the wardrobes of millions of men. But from the perspective of actual consumer buying patterns, a blazer in an atypical size actually has more in common with a fashion-driven product than with the same style jacket in a popular size. For example, sales for 46-regular, one of the most popular sizes, vary only by twice the average weekly demand, while sales for 43-regular vary as much as four times the average demand. A rare size, such as 43-long, would vary even more. (See the exhibit "The Importance of SKU-Level Analysis.") To satisfy retail customers, the manufacturer must hold a proportionately larger inventory of 43-regular, even though in absolute terms it will hold much more of 46-regular. But most manufacturers, including this one, tend to assign the same inventory policy for all products in a product line.

By fine-tuning inventories according to SKU-level demand, a manufacturer can increase profits and reduce inventory risks. To demonstrate that improvement, we ran a computer simulation that tests various inventory policies for three groups of SKUs in the same product line—one group with low variance in demand, another with medium variance, and the third with high variance. (See the exhibit "A Better Way to Manage Inventory.")

The first test shows a scenario in which a manufacturer is most concerned about keeping its big retail customers happy by maintaining very high order fulfillment rates. The manufacturer sets a single inventory policy to ensure that its highest variance SKUs have plenty of finished goods on hand—say nine times the expected weekly demand for those SKUs. Following that inventory policy, the other two groups of SKUs in that product line also carry inventory of nine times the expected weekly demand even though their variation is never more than four times the average.

The second test reflects a manufacturer whose concern is maintaining inventories at a level appropriate for its high-volume, low-variability SKUs—say three weeks of demand. That means much lower inventories in general and a savings in working capital and risk. But the trade-off is that the manufacturer frequently runs short on its medium- and especially its high-variability items. That means lost sales and maybe a canceled contract with a prized customer.

In the third test, the manufacturer focuses on balancing the costs of stock-outs and inventory by setting a single inventory policy for all SKUs at seven weeks. In the case of blazers, the inventory of the 43-regular is just about right, but there are too many 46-regulars and stockouts of 43-longs.

The better approach, of course, is for the manufacturer to assign an individual inventory policy for each

The Importance of SKU-Level Analysis

The inventory demand for SKUs within the same product line can vary significantly. These charts show the weekly demand across more than a thousand retail outlets for one style of men's blazer in two different sizes. The top chart shows the demand for 46-regular, which is one of the most popular sizes. The bottom does the same for 43-regular, a much slower-selling size. To high-light the variation in demand, we've expressed the sales numbers in units of weekly demand. While 46-regular sells a lot more

Blazer, Size 46-Regular

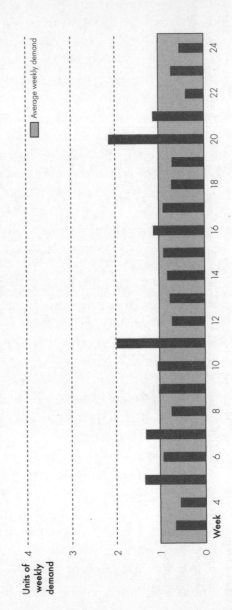

than 43-regular, those sales are relatively stable—peak sales are only about twice the weekly average. Sales for 43-regular vary a lot more—up to four times the weekly average. As a result, the manufacturer has to keep a much bigger inventory of 43-regular, relative to average weekly sales, than it does for 46-regular. If we were looking at 43-long, the inventory would be bigger still. Although this type of analysis can be done on a simple spreadsheet, manufacturers generally ignore this variation and assign the same inventory targets for all SKUs in the product line.

Blazer, Size 43-Regular

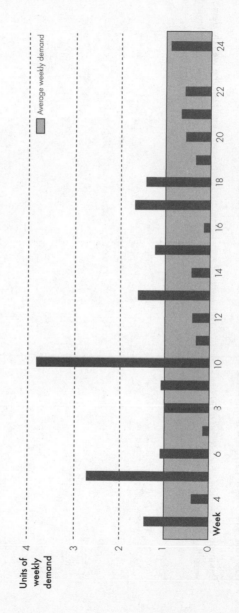

Units of weekly demand

Average weekly demand

Week

A Better Way to Manage Inventory

This table shows the effects of different inventory policies on a set of three SKUs within a product line. The first case focuses on achieving very high order fulfillment for all products to satisfy demanding retailers, but at the cost of high inventories. The second focuses on meeting demand for high-volume products, and the third seeks to maximize profits by balancing the costs of stockouts and inventory. In each of these cases, a single inventory policy is set for all three SKU groups. The fourth case sets inventory policies appropriate for each SKU, maximizing profits while reducing inventory risks.

	Sales	Production costs	Inventory costs	Average order-fulfillment ratio	Total Inventory (Weeks of demand)	Profit
1. Minimize stockouts (Single inventory policy)	$1,761	$1,198	$79	97%	18	$485
2. Minimize inventory costs (Single inventory policy)	$1,612	$1,062	$55	89%	13	$494
3. Balance stockout and inventory costs (Single inventory policy)	$1,739	$1,158	$70	95%	16	$512
4. Maximize profits and reduce inventory risk (SKU-level inventory policy)	$1,728	$1,148	$66	95%	15	$515

Dollar amounts are weekly, in thousands

SKU. The fourth test optimizes the profit of each SKU according to the estimated costs of stocking out versus holding inventory. Inventories for some SKUs go up, while others go down, but overall inventories fall. And net profits rise.

We know of no manufacturers that have fully implemented what we propose. Yet lean retailers like Home Depot and Wal-Mart already incorporate some SKU-level analysis in their own inventory decision making. Calculating SKU-level variation can be done on a simple spreadsheet, so moving toward this type of inventory policy should be quite feasible.

Rethinking Your Sourcing Strategy

SKU-level analysis has big implications for sourcing as well. For a long time, manufacturers focused on direct costs when they located factories. As a result, many shifted production to developing countries, where labor costs are low. Lately, partly in reaction to the pressures of lean retailing, they've learned the importance of delivering certain goods quickly to the marketplace, so they've moved some production closer to home. In the 1990s, for example, the American apparel manufacturers shifted a full third of the industry's sourcing from Asia to Mexico and the Caribbean. And finally, U.S. manufacturers have experimented with flexible production lines within a factory that allow for fast changeover to make hot-selling lines. But all of these sourcing strategies still tend to treat all SKUs within a product line the same. A better approach would be to move low-volume, high-variance SKUs close to markets, while producing most high-volume, low-variance goods offshore where it is most cost effective.

To set an optimal sourcing policy for a product line, the first step once again is to determine each SKU's variability. Next, arrange the SKUs into groups with similar variations in weekly demand. Each group will have separate inventory policies, and the allocation among different plants will depend on capacity, capabilities, production costs, and lead times for each plant, as well as profit margins.

To simulate this decision, we took the same portfolio of three groups of SKUs as before. The manufacturer has two sourcing options. The offshore facility has low costs but, at 11 weeks, a long lead time for production. The domestic "short-cycle" factory takes only two weeks to bring products to market, but its direct manufacturing costs are 20% higher. The results for this case appear in the exhibit "Sourcing at the SKU Level," which shows how assigning different percentages of total production to the two sources affects profitability and inventory position of the manufacturer.

At one extreme, the manufacturer decides to minimize direct production costs, so it assigns all production offshore. At the other extreme, it uses only the short-cycle line in order to minimize lead time and inventories. The intermediate cases represent a mix of the two facilities, where most of the high variance SKUs are made at the short-cycle plant, while most of the low-variance SKUs go offshore.

Our simulation reveals that the mixed strategy yields the highest profits while still reducing exposure to total inventory risk. The simulation looks explicitly at inventory levels as well as profits, which brings to the forefront both the considerable risk of inventory obsolescence as well as the return on different sourcing strategies. The higher the valuation of inventory risk, the more desirable the short-cycle option becomes. The simulation results show that inventory exposure decreases dramatically as the manufacturer draws more on the short-cycle option. And note that as the number of SKUs increases, so does the demand variability for the manufacturer. While the

---

Sourcing at the SKU Level

This graph shows the effects of sourcing decisions on profitability and inventory risk. It simulates the scenario of a manufacturer with two factories: an offshore plant with an 11-week lead time and a higher-cost, short-cycle plant with a two-week lead time. The graph shows how profits (the solid line) vary as the manufacturer draws on more production capacity from the short-cycle plant. At one extreme, all production is made at the overseas factory, thereby minimizing production costs. At the other extreme, the short-cycle plant handles everything, thereby minimizing inventory costs. The intermediate values represent a mix of the two facilities, where most of the low-variance SKUs are made offshore and the high-variance SKUs are made at the short-cycle plant. A mixed strategy actually has higher profitability than the 100% offshore option as well as substantially lower inventory costs. The greater the valuation of the inventory risk, the closer the manufacturer will move toward the 100% short-cycle option.

Impact of Short-Cycle Manufacturing on Profits and Inventory

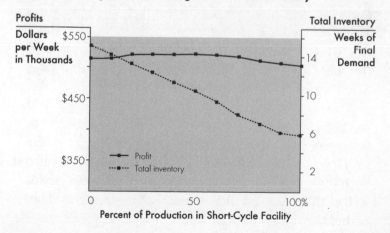

Percent of Production in Short-Cycle Facility

offshore option remains the most desirable for the lowest-variation SKUs, product proliferation raises the value of the option to produce closer to the market.

In this light, manufacturers would do well to look at their product lines as portfolios of distinct goods. In satisfying the demand of retailers for differentiated products, manufacturers must evaluate the risk that comes with producing the different items in their offerings. By conducting SKU-level analysis, companies can understand the true risks and returns associated with each item, and manage them accordingly.

Product Proliferation in the Book Industry

THE BOOK INDUSTRY MAY SEEM a world apart from other consumer goods. But it illustrates what happens when radical product proliferation—more than 1.2 million individual titles in print—combines with extremely high fixed costs for each batch of production. The weekly demand for an average book, if it could be charted, would vary far beyond anything discussed here. As a result, most manufacturers continue to produce books in big batches, based largely on advance retail orders. But book retailers have begun to adopt many features of lean retailing and also some aspects of SKU-level inventory policies. Manufacturers are likely to follow suit.

To minimize their own inventories, most bookstores offer three kinds of availability to consumers. A hot new book, such as a novel by a major writer, is likely to be stacked high on display tables. But a similar novel by a first-time author may not be. The store will hold only one or two copies of that book. If it runs out of the book, the store can get a copy from the distributor fairly quickly. And what about the previously best-selling novel that everyone's now forgotten? The book is still in print, but the bookstore won't bother keeping any copies on hand. If a customer wants a copy, the store requests one directly from the distributor or publisher, who delivers the book in a few weeks. You can see this type of SKU-level differentiation explicitly at Amazon.com. Books are listed as usually shipping within 24 hours, in two to three days, or in one to two weeks.

As the lean retailing practices of bookstores intensify, distributors and publishers are likely to come under pressure to hold bigger inventories and improve their response to orders. What can they do about it? They can rethink their sourcing strategies. We can see the future in booktech.com, an upstart company that uses digital printing technology. Already popular for customized textbooks and course packets, this printing process is the epitome of flexible manufacturing: it can provide booksellers with rapid replenishment of small orders, but eliminates the need to carry inventories. As production efficiencies for this process continue to improve—and as book publishers work on reducing their own costly inventories—we expect more and more books to be printed this way. Books from major writers will continue to be printed in large batches, but slower-selling books will be printed on demand. As in other industries, this differentiation strategy will allow publishers to meet the needs of retailers while managing exposure to inventory risk.

Originally published in November–December 2000
Reprint R00601

Your Loyalty Program Is Betraying You

JOSEPH C. NUNES AND XAVIER DRÈZE

Executive Summary

EVEN AS LOYALTY PROGRAMS are launched left and right, many are being scuttled. How can that be? These days, everyone knows that an old customer retained is worth more than a new customer won. What is so hard about making a simple loyalty program work?

Quite a lot, the authors say. The biggest challenges include clarifying business goals, engineering the reward structure, and creating incentives powerful enough to change buying behavior but not so generous that they erode margins. Additionally, companies have to sort out the puzzles of consumer psychology, which can result, for example, in two rewards of equal economic value inspiring very different levels of purchasing.

In their research, the authors have discovered patterns in what the successful loyalty programs get right and in how the others fall. Together, their findings constitute a tool kit for designing something rare indeed: a program that won't do you wrong.

To begin with, it's important to know exactly what a loyalty program can do. It can keep customers from defecting, induce them to consolidate certain purchases with one seller (in other words, win a greater share of wallet), prompt customers to make additional purchases, yield insight into their behavior and preferences, and turn a profit. A program can meet these objectives in several ways—for instance, by offering rewards (points, say, or frequent-flier miles) divisible enough to provide many redemption opportunities but not so divisible that they fail to lock in customers.

Companies striving to generate customer loyalty should avoid five common mistakes: Don't create a new commodity, which can result in price wars and other tit-for-tat competitive moves; don't cater to the disloyal by making rewards easy for just anyone to reap; don't reward purchasing volume over profitability; don't give away the store; and, finally, don't promise what can't be delivered.

WHAT IS MORE RARE THAN undying loyalty? Apparently, an undying loyalty program. In the past few years, we've seen companies of all kinds killing off the programs they'd designed to inspire greater fidelity in the ranks of customers. Subway, the restaurant chain, got rid of its Sub Club cards, which allowed diners to earn a free sandwich after purchasing eight. In Australia, Coles supermarkets phased out a program that rewarded owners of the company's stock with merchandise discounts ranging from 3% to 7.5%. Online phenomenon eBay quietly pulled the plug on its Anything Points program for U.S. customers. Target missed the mark, it seems, with its innovative approach involving "smart" credit cards. American Airlines and America Online jettisoned their joint customer-loyalty program. The list goes on. Even as loyalty programs are launched left and right, many are being scuttled, and not with a sense of mission accomplished.

How can this be? In many cases, these programs are created by highly competent marketers in otherwise successful businesses. It is now well recognized that an old customer retained is worth more than a new customer won. The concept of rewarding frequent buyers has been around to tinker with at least since the days of the Green Stamp. What could be so hard about a simple loyalty program?

After researching that question in various ways over the past several years, we've learned that there are many aspects of loyalty programs that are hard to get right. The challenges start with clarifying business goals, given that loyalty programs can produce a variety of benefits. They continue with engineering the economics of reward structure and creating incentives good enough to change behavior but not so generous that they erode margins. Not least, there are puzzles of consumer psychology to sort out, which can make two rewards of equal value inspire very different levels of purchasing.

Our research suggests that there are patterns in what the successful loyalty programs get right and in how the others fail. In this article, we share what we have learned conducting our own studies and observing programs in practice. Together, our findings constitute a tool kit for designing something rare indeed: a program that won't do you wrong.

What Can a Loyalty Program Reasonably Do?

Creating a successful loyalty program starts with defining what should be gained from the effort. Only with clear business goals can one design the appropriate mechanisms and judge whether they are operating effectively. So let's take note, first of all, of what a loyalty program cannot do. It cannot, in any true sense, create loyalty. "Loyalty" means faithfulness. It means unswerving devotion. If you are loyal to something—a concept, a person, a product—you are not a fair-weather friend. You stick with it even when doing so runs counter to your interests. But surely this is not something to be expected in any commercial setting; it's scarce enough in love and war.

We don't raise this semantic issue facetiously or with a sense of outrage. Rather, our point is that euphemisms, especially ones as broadly adopted as "customer loyalty," don't make the work of management easier. They muddy the waters and throw marketing efforts off course.

To clarify things, then, let's explore the five goals loyalty programs really can serve.

KEEP CUSTOMERS FROM DEFECTING

In some cases, loyalty programs create what marketers call barriers to exit. That is, they make it hard for customers to switch to new vendors. This is a critical goal in situations where customers typically use only one supplier, as with mobile phone service or home heating oil. Given the high stakes of a customer's lifetime value, the focus is on keeping accounts from falling into enemy hands.

Take, for example, this reward to Sprint's long-distance phone customers: For every dollar they spend with Sprint, they earn an airline mile redeemable with any of five different airlines. Sprint rival AT&T does not offer such a plan. Consequently, all else being equal, a member of any of those five airlines' frequent-flier programs would rather have Sprint as a long-distance carrier. A customer might stick with Sprint even if she became temporarily dissatisfied with the service, because the mileage benefit accrues over time. If she left and later came back, she would have to start accruing miles all over again. This is what's known as lock-in—the customer's equivalent of an employee's "golden handcuffs."

WIN GREATER SHARE OF WALLET

For goods and services a customer typically buys from more than one seller, a loyalty program can encourage the consolidation of purchases. This applies to air travel, groceries, credit, food and drink, gasoline—all purchases made frequently and in small amounts. The key is to give the customer a reason to steer more of that business into one seller's hands.

Awarding points for purchases is the most common way of doing this. For example, Amazon.com offers a Visa card that rewards shoppers with a point, worth a penny, for every dollar they spend (three points if the dollar goes toward an Amazon purchase), distributed in the form of a $25 Amazon gift certificate when 2,500 points are accumulated. A shopper who might otherwise alternate among stores now has a reason to favor Amazon. Indeed, even if another seller offers a similar program, there is an incentive to consolidate in one place because certificates are issued once a threshold of points has been reached. Many such programs exist in the credit industry, and for good reason: In 2004, the 185 million credit card holders in America each carried an average of four cards. Of course, points programs are used far beyond the world of credit cards. Retail stores and hotels, for instance, also use them—witness Best Buy's Reward Zone program and Starwood's Preferred Guest program, a favorite of business travelers.

If we had any doubts about how effectively a program could increase share of wallet, they were dispelled by Arizona retailer ABCO's success in capturing more of its customers' purchases of baby goods. The Baby Club we helped launch rewarded members with Baby Bucks for purchases; 100 Baby Bucks could be exchanged for a $10 voucher. Within six months, we observed a substantial uptick in the number of transactions involving baby products and in the average number of baby products per transaction, adding up to a 25% net increase in baby product sales. This increase did not occur because there was a sudden baby boom. It was purely the result of parents' driving past competitors to consolidate their baby-related purchases at ABCO.

Of course, the Baby Club was able to achieve such results because it was the first program of its kind in the area. For most companies in competitive markets, that's at best an ephemeral advantage. But even where there are competing programs, it is possible to prevail with the right reward structure. Specifically, your program should feature what economists call a convex reward structure, whereby greater levels of expenditure earn proportionately greater rewards. Homebase, the UK do-it-yourself retailer, has arrived at a two-tiered system that seems to work: Customers save 2% on purchases as soon as they become members of the Spend & Save program. Once they've spent £400, they save 10% on the rest of their purchases that year. Consider the incentive that creates for a homeowner who spends about £800 per year on DIY supplies. If he splits his purchases evenly between Homebase and one of its competitors (spending £400 at each outlet), he receives £8 back from each retailer (assuming that the competitor has a similar program), for a total of £16 in savings. But if he spends the entire £800 at Homebase, he receives £48 back.

PROMPT CUSTOMERS TO MAKE ADDITIONAL PURCHASES

We've been describing situations where competing for a customer's purchases is a zero-sum game. The expectation is that the customer will buy just so much and no more, and the objective is to capture the largest portion of that amount. But a loyalty program needn't set its sights so low; it can also create incremental demand, spurring purchases that would not otherwise be made.

This is a common effect of multitiered loyalty programs (those with, say, Silver, Gold, and Platinum levels), where each tier brings additional benefits. Customers who are on the cusp of attaining the next status level—or in danger of slipping to a lower one—will often spend more in order to secure the higher ground. To cite one of the most extreme examples we've seen: A friend of ours in Los Angeles found himself 3,000 miles short of United Air Lines' Premier Executive status with just a few weeks remaining in 2005. He took the least expensive qualifying flight, to the frigid destination of Buffalo, New York, where he stayed less than 24 hours before returning.

Even when status levels are not part of a program, a valued reward can lead consumers to accelerate their purchases, and that can add up to increased overall consumption. Working with a chain of car washes on the West Coast, we observed that a loyalty program offering a free wash after eight purchases led drivers to wash their cars more often as they got closer and closer to earning the reward. This same effect has been observed by other researchers studying coffee shop purchases, and it would no doubt apply to small luxuries like tanning and spa sessions, as well. The common thread is that these are goods and services for which consumption is flexible and can be increased easily. A service station might therefore create a reward program for oil changes and see overall sales rise; using it for snow tire changeovers probably would not work out as well.

YIELD INSIGHT INTO CUSTOMER BEHAVIOR AND PREFERENCES

A benefit of loyalty programs that has gained prominence in the past decade is their ability to provide useful data about customers. The data can both produce insights about general buying behavior and allow the seller to target promotions to individual customers. Tesco, the UK grocery store chain, is often cited for its expertise in using the data collected from its Clubcard members. Cardholders receive a quarterly mailing with offers so carefully customized that Clive Humby, one of Clubcard's architects, told *Promo* magazine in 2004 that Tesco prints about 4 million variations for each mailing. As data collection and maintenance become easier and cheaper, we are witnessing a proliferation of companies offering to provide marketing insights based on loyalty program data.

Yet one must be careful not to overstate the benefits of collecting consumer purchase data. Initiatives like

Tesco's require a dedicated staff of analysts and substantial investments in data management and augmentation. And even then, a company's customer data, taken in isolation, may not yield many novel insights. We were reminded of this when we worked with Twentieth Century Fox Home Entertainment. Few would suspect that online purchasers of X-Men movies would be prime targets for 1930s-era Shirley Temple movies. But indeed, we discovered that action film fans with kids were especially receptive to pitches for the young actress's movies. How could Fox Home Entertainment determine which of its customers had children? Only by combining its own data with information purchased from third-party provider Equifax. The point is, it isn't sufficient to collect loyalty program data and expect that effective marketing moves will spontaneously suggest themselves; one must have a marketing objective in mind and then seek the data.

TURN A PROFIT

Some loyalty programs can even function as profit centers. Consider American Airlines' AAdvantage program. Even as the airline racks up billions of dollars in debt, the AAdvantage program turns a tidy profit selling miles to other businesses to use as rewards for their customers. AAdvantage clients range from huge concerns like Citibank to small businesses like Ariake, a sushi restaurant in Los Angeles. Consumers of Kellogg's breakfast cereals get thanked with American Airlines miles; so do subscribers to *USA Today*. Together, U.S. based airlines sell nearly $2 billion worth of miles to more than 22,000 businesses.

This may seem like a loyalty program's crowning achievement, a gambit available only to the long established and mature. In fact, it was the function of the earliest broad-based program, S&H Green Stamps. Thomas Sperry (the "S" in "S&H") did not create Green Stamps in 1896 to reward customers of a business S&H owned. The system was conceived as an independent business that would sell stamps to merchants, along with the books to paste them in. S&H's only direct trade with consumers was through redemption centers where people exchanged their stamps for merchandise.

Today, any company with a broad customer base and excess capacity could consider leveraging its loyalty program in the same way. Marriott has done so with its Rewards program, enabling customers to collect points for a future hotel stay by shopping at Target, the Gap, Lands' End, Macy's, or Best Buy. But of course, these types of ventures, while generating additional revenues, also involve all the complexity of running stand-alone businesses. A critical concern is arriving at the right price per reward point. In the airline business, for example, the average mile sells for about two cents, although it goes for significantly less to high-volume customers like Citibank. This means the airline sells the right to 25,000 miles for about $500 in incremental revenue. In most businesses, economics like this would be disastrous, but airlines are able to keep the true incremental costs quite low. They can limit the availability of qualifying seats, and they count on a certain portion of miles going unredeemed. If food, beverage, fuel, reservations processing, liability insurance, and other miscellaneous expenses are factored in, the 25,000-mile reward actually costs less than $15, on average, to fulfill.

We've outlined five benefits a company can gain from a loyalty program, and the corollary should be clear: Any given program must be designed to serve specific goals, and priorities must be set among them. It's unreasonable to expect to design a program that equally pursues several distinct objectives. Rather, it makes sense to focus on a couple and design the optimal program to serve them. (If additional benefits can then be layered onto that design, fine—but only if that can be done without compromising performance in the key areas.) The unfortunate reality, however, is that many loyalty programs seem to have no distinct targets squarely in their sights.

The Levers of Loyalty

On the face of it, designing a loyalty program is a straightforward exercise. It must be attractive to customers and not too expensive. Both sides of that equation, however, are easier said than done. Our study of programs in practice suggests that several components are especially important and difficult to design well.

DIVISIBILITY OF REWARDS

First, there is a careful balance to strike in what we would term "divisibility," or the number of discrete reward-redemption opportunities a program provides. A program that allows members to redeem points in clusters of 5,000 is twice as divisible as one that allows people to redeem points only in clusters of 10,000. Managers and their customers often diverge in their preferences on this matter. Customers prefer highly divisible programs because they provide many exchange opportunities and thus reduce award waste. They see a low-divisibility program as having such a high threshold for rewards that it deters them from ever embarking on the quest. By contrast, managers don't like offering highly divisible programs because they are not effective at creating consumer lock-in. If one can redeem 5,000 points, why strive to accumulate 10,000? As always is the case when the desires of companies and those of consumers collide, a compromise must be struck. The right level of divisibility will factor in the expected yearly program usage and the amount of company differentiation. Our research shows, for example, that in a grocery store setting (high usage, low differentiation), a $50 reward for every $500 spent engenders greater customer loyalty than either a $10 reward for every $100 spent or a $100 reward for every $1,000 spent (too much and too little divisibility, respectively).

SENSE OF MOMENTUM

Research has proven that the further along members are in a loyalty program, the more they use it. By contrast, at the outset of their membership, their involvement is irresolute. Because they have not yet made any progress, the rewards seem far away. Worse, they have little sense of how easy it will be to achieve the goals. Rather than lose a customer's interest right out of the gate, the best designed programs provide what we've termed "endowed progress," a little push to get things moving. We learned how effective endowed progress can be when we staged a field experiment at a metropolitan car wash. (See the exhibit "The Effect of a Jump Start" for details.)

Let us quickly offer a caveat, however. Customers must see the endowment as earned or warranted by their behavior, or the tactic will have little effect. Indeed, if it smacks of cynicism, it may produce a negative one. Even if the endowed progress is simply cast as a signing bonus for new program members, it should give them a sense of established momentum.

NATURE OF REWARDS

Research about the compensation of professional sales-people has shown that they respond more dramatically to performance incentives that promise pleasure (like luxe vacations and, in decades past, fur coats) than to purely utilitarian incentives (like cash bonuses). In the same way, consumers love to be given a treat they would not splurge on with their own money. And so the most successful loyalty programs often feature less functional and more pleasure-providing rewards. When Maritz Loyalty Marketing, which operates loyalty programs for various merchants, analyzed the reward redemptions for its clients in 2005, it found that American consumers preferred the latest electronics (televisions, video games, stereos, DVD players) to household goods (appliances, furniture, art) by a factor of almost two to one. But the benefit of offering nonutilitarian rewards is not simply that they get people excited about the program. In experiencing the reward, people come to have pleasant associations with the brand. Note what happened with Nectar, a UK-based reward program that serves customers of various retail outlets. Its members collected more points (in other words, spent more at program-affiliated stores) during the month immediately following a point redemption than during other months—and the effect was even greater when the points were redeemed for a hedonic reward such as theme park admission.

American Express Incentive Services is well aware of this element in its program design. It divides rewards into two types: sticky and slippery. Sticky rewards stick

The Effect of a Jump Start

In April 2004, we staged an experiment in a car wash business in Los Angeles. The business distributed 300 stampable cards that promised a free car wash after eight paid visits. The cards, however, took two forms. Card 1 was a straightforward buy-eight-get-one offer. Card 2 presented itself as a buy-ten-get-one offer, but customers were told that, as a special promotion, they were being given the first two stamps free. Essentially, then, the economics of the two programs were identical. The question was whether those two stamps, by framing the quest as one that had been undertaken rather than one not yet begun, would have an effect on sales.

The "endowed progress effect," as we termed it, turned out to be substantial. First, total redemptions were higher. While only 19% of the customers with Card 1 stuck with the program and claimed the prize, 34% of Card 2 customers did so. Card 2 customers also came back at a faster rate, as reflected in the diagrams (which represent only the customers who got all their stamps and earned the free wash). As this comparison shows, the average elapsed time between visits was less for Card 2 than for Card 1. Finally, under both programs, purchasing accelerated: The time between visits became shorter and shorter as the customer got closer to the payoff. But note that the rate of acceleration was greater with Card 2. The time between visits compressed more along the way.

For details on this study, see our article "The Endowed Progress Effect" in the March 2006 issue of the Journal of Consumer Research.

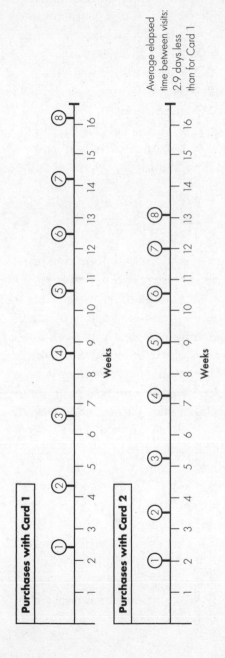

Purchases with Card 1

Weeks
1 2 3 4 5 6 7 8 9 10 11 12 13 14 15 16

① ② ③ ④ ⑤ ⑥ ⑦ ⑧

Purchases with Card 2

Weeks
1 2 3 4 5 6 7 8 9 10 11 12 13 14 15 16

① ② ③ ④ ⑤ ⑥ ⑦ ⑧

Average elapsed
time between visits:
2.9 days less
than for Card 1

in the recipient's mind, reinforcing the relationship with the program provider, while slippery rewards are mundane and tend to slip from memory. Which do you think is stickier: the utilitarian reward that's quickly assimilated into the recipient's daily life, or the reward that breaks the routine and may even confer bragging rights? Hoping for stickier rewards, American Express has launched its In:Chicago and In:LA specialty cards, which allow members in Chicago or Los Angeles to earn "special dining, drinking, and entertainment rewards at some of the city's best spots."

EXPANSION OF RELATIONSHIP

Sometimes, the only effect of a buy-ten-get-one-free program is to give away a product unnecessarily. After all, a customer who likes a product enough to buy it ten times could probably be expected to purchase it again. By making the 11th time free, the company effectively gives the habitual buyer a quantity discount. (Subway's Sub Club used to do exactly this.) More valuable to a company is a program that expands the consumer's repertoire of purchases. For example, instead of giving an 11th cup free, a coffee shop might make the tenth a larger size or throw in a free pastry. As well as being a more hedonic reward, the sample might introduce the consumer to a new product and induce higher future sales. This is one reason airlines are happy to fill empty seats in business or first class with members spending frequent-flier miles for an upgrade. It gives the traveler the taste of a better experience that he might find difficult to live without in the future. In fact, Subway's current plans are to offer franchises a new reward program, featuring a magnetic card that will allow customers to trade points for cookies and other extras.

COMBINED-CURRENCY FLEXIBILITY

A program in which consumers never redeem points would be very inexpensive to offer. However, it would be of little interest to members. To be attractive, a program must lead to redemption; that's when the benefits really become the most salient to the consumer. The key for managers is to make the redemption as inexpensive as possible to the company. In our research, we have found that if companies allow program members to redeem their points in combination with hard currency, it lowers the psychological cost to consumers. In other words, it can increase the perceived benefit to the consumer without undue cost to the company.

For example, we found that consumers would rather buy a flight with $250 and a copayment of 5,000 frequent-flier miles than with a straight payment of either $300 or 30,000 miles. Small amounts of miles seem trivial to the consumer, as they make most mileage rewards seem too far away. Thus, being able to spend these alternative currencies in smaller amounts (accompanied by cash) is more appealing than spending lots of precious miles on a cheap flight. An expensive flight, however, is another story. (See the exhibit "The Case for Currency Combinations.") More simply put, companies stand to gain incremental sales when they're flexible in how they allow customers to combine currencies.

Mistakes to Avoid

We've been reviewing the finer points of loyalty program design—the elements that, when carefully managed, separate the best programs from mediocre or bad ones. It's easy to come away from such research with the strong sense that the devil is in the details. But in truth, when we reflect on the programs that were outright failures, we see that the issues were not all that nuanced. Loyalty programs typically founder on some simple mistakes. Allow us to offer five basic pieces of advice.

DON'T CREATE A NEW COMMODITY

If your program is tantamount to discounting, then you are only paying people to buy and, paradoxically, creat-

---

The Case for Currency Combinations

Some points-based loyalty programs allow customers to combine points with cash to pay for purchases. For instance, a Net SAAver fare advertised on American Airlines' Web site allowed fliers to purchase any ticket normally priced at $189 either for $189 or for $39 plus 16,000 miles.

To discover how consumers respond to such combined-currency prices, we asked airline travelers who had experience with miles programs to look at a hypothetical set of pricing options. We presented two scenarios, asking some participants to consider a low-cost flight and others to consider a high-cost flight. For each case, respondents were asked to choose among payment options of all miles, all cash, or a combination of the two. Our respondents in the low-cost scenario could pay for a $300 flight ($250 plus a $50 surcharge for expedited booking) with cash or with 30,000 miles or with a combination of, say, $250 and 5,000 miles. Respondents in the high-cost scenario could pay for a $1,000 flight and a $50 surcharge with $1,050 or with 105,000 miles or with a combination of money and miles.

In pure economic terms, all the options cost the same. But as the charts show, preferences ended up varying based on the cost of the flight. For the low-cost flight, people preferred a combined-currency payment. For the high-cost flight, people preferred a single-currency transaction. In our article "Using Combined-Currency Prices to Lower Consumers' Perceived Cost" (Journal of Marketing Research, February 2004), we model the marginal values being placed on miles by consumers and suggest how merchants can optimize their pricing accordingly. For here, it is sufficient to say that consumers do prefer combined-currency pricing under some conditions, and a program with the flexibility to offer it will be more successful than one without that flexibility.

ing greater disloyalty. You will inevitably be drawn into the equivalent of a price war, with tit-for-tat competitive moves basically yielding parity and lower profitability all around. Just consider the attempt last August by United Air Lines to poach fliers worried about a mechanics' strike at Northwest Airlines. In an e-mail promotion, United targeted customers in certain midwestern cities with an offer of double miles. Northwest responded by matching the offer for flights taken before early October. In mid-October, United announced it would award double miles for travel until mid-December. All of this had the opposite effect of what either side wanted—it encouraged price shopping.

Low-Cost Scenario

A flight worth $250, with a $50 surcharge.
How would you prefer to pay?

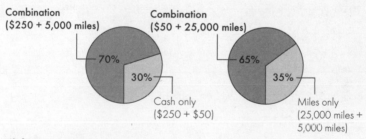

Combination
($250 + 5,000 miles)

70%

30%

Cash only
($250 + $50)

Combination
($50 + 25,000 miles)

65%

35%

Miles only
(25,000 miles +
5,000 miles)

High-Cost Scenario

A flight worth $1,000, with a $50 surcharge.
How would you prefer to pay?

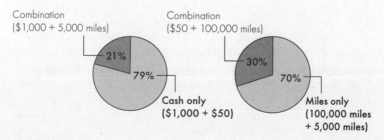

Combination
($1,000 + 5,000 miles)

21%

79%

Cash only
($1,000 + $50)

Combination
($50 + 100,000 miles)

30%

70%

Miles only
(100,000 miles
+ 5,000 miles)

It's worth noting that the same thing killed the Green Stamp. Stores began trying to outdo one another by offering double stamps, then triple stamps, and ultimately quadruple stamps, inflating the value of the average stamp to about eight cents on the dollar. Shoppers were happy to go wherever they could collect the most stamps. What had begun as a mechanism for rewarding loyal customers devolved into clumsily concealed price promotions administered by third-party stamp providers. Eventually, stores had had enough and began touting the benefit of lower prices with no stamps attached.

The thought of offering double miles, points, or credits to steal share in the short term is compelling. Almost all loyalty programs, from Best Western's Gold Crown Club to Hilton's HHonors, and from American Express Rewards to Visa Extras, have at one time or another upped the amount of the alternative currency they offer in exchange for sales. But managers must use their loyalty programs for more than a direct payment mechanism for purchases, which is simply not sustainable in the long term.

DON'T REWARD THE DISLOYAL

Probably the most familiar example of a program that rewards the unfaithful is the typical grocery store card. Beyond their data-gathering purpose, these cards are meant to attract customers by giving members-only discounts on promotion items. Card-carrying shoppers get the advantages of coupons without having to clip them. Because no store charges for membership, though, shoppers quickly accumulate as many cards as there are local grocers. This type of program does not reward loyal behavior; it rewards card ownership. And sometimes it doesn't even do that, because helpful cashiers are often happy to swipe a dummy card for customers who have forgotten or never signed up for their own.

Therefore, managers must ensure that their loyalty programs are incentive compatible, designed so it is in customers' best interests to be loyal. A program should reward the use of the card over time rather than on a given purchase occasion, and it should discriminate between more and less loyal customers in the size of its rewards. For example, at the women's clothing chain Chico's, customers become Passport members after spending $500, entitling them to discounts and targeted communications.

DON'T REWARD VOLUME OVER PROFITABILITY

Gauging loyalty solely on the basis of such rudimentary measures as purchase quantity can be very misleading. Instead, Harrah's Entertainment, for instance, tracks the types of gambling that people do and focuses on its most profitable customers. Its loyalty program recognizes, for example, that roulette wheels have a different house take than slot machines. Thus, when a customer calls to book a night at one of its properties, Harrah's is able to generate a spot price for the room based on customer profitability as well as availability. Profitable customers might stay for free while others might be charged hundreds of dollars for the same room or even be told that no rooms are available.

Frequent-flier programs are beginning to follow suit. American Airlines revamped its entire AAdvantage system to track members according to their profitability. The program still adheres to the convention of issuing miles to fliers but can use the customer's P&L when making other decisions about the customer relationship.

Keeping track of the profitability of the customers is paramount. Companies reward loyalty because they believe it leads to profits. By tracking profits directly, a company can better target its rewards.

DON'T GIVE AWAY THE STORE

There's no reason to cut into profit margins if a customer can be made happy with a costless reward. For example, United Air Lines ranks meal service in its first and business classes based on seniority. A 1K cardholder is asked her choice of entrée before a Premier or Premier Executive cardholder. It costs the airline nothing to bestow this honor, because the numbers and types of meals taken on board do not change. Similarly, Citibank does not answer the customer service calls it receives in the order they are received; rather, wait time is a function of the callers' assets. Many managers refer to this type of preferential treatment as customer recognition. Call it what you like—it effectively rewards the most valuable customers.

Even if managers cannot make customer rewards costless, they can often lower the costs. A classic way to achieve this is to provide coupons rather than straight discounts. Baby Club's 10% discount, for example, was given in the form of Baby Bucks that could be redeemed for $10 vouchers that themselves could be redeemed for groceries at ABCO. When interviewed, club members showed real enthusiasm for the "10% discount" they received. However, when we looked at the liability to the store, we found that the low redemption rate coupled with the profit margin on the sales of the items bought with the coupons reduced the liability from 10% to a mere 1.72%.

DON'T PROMISE WHAT YOU CAN'T DELIVER

When a loyalty program pledges to reward customers with preferential treatment (shorter lines, expedited delivery, special toll-free numbers), it must ensure that the services provided through these special arrangements are better than the services available to regular customers. This is particularly true when customers can easily compare the two levels of service. While it may be hard to gauge the amount of time others spend waiting on the phone, it is easy to see whether the first-class ticket line moves faster than the regular line. Comparison is especially salient when customers are waiting for their luggage. The premier passenger cannot help but observe how many bags without a bright orange or pink "priority" tag are delivered before he gets his.

To make matters worse, customers do not compare averages with averages; they compare extremes with extremes. That is, they notice the speed of service only when they are not being served promptly. Our research suggests that, on average, airline luggage marked as "priority" tends to come out of the plane faster. Many airlines even have a special container for these bags. Yet we have also found that, frequently, a good number of nonpriority bags are delivered before the last priority bag comes out. If too many nonpriority bags are delivered before priority bags, the premier passenger begins believing that the promise of superior service has been broken. Managers need to ensure that the lower bounds of premium service never look worse than standard service.

Keep the Faith

We began this article with a litany of failures, a sampling of loyalty programs that were dumped for not delivering. In a way, this is the good news, because many other programs that should get canceled continue to limp along.

Yet loyalty programs are ingenious marketing tools when they are designed and executed well. In a wide variety of industry settings, they've proven their ability to reduce churn, increase sales and profitability, and yield the kind of insight that allows a company to provide more valued service to its customers.

Making sure that a company's loyalty program will carry its weight begins with clarifying what the program is expected to do. This requires careful attention to the details of program design, from the value and nature of the rewards to the ways in which they are bestowed and redeemed. Perhaps more than anything, a successful program depends on competent and consistent execution. Even with all of this, true loyalty might be too much to expect, but companies will likely have longer-term relationships with happier customers. And that, to us, sounds like the best kind of competitive advantage.

Originally published in April 2006
Reprint R0604H

Localization

The Revolution in Consumer Markets

DARRELL K. RIGBY AND
VIJAY VISHWANATH

Executive Summary

STANDARDIZATION HAS BEEN a powerful strategy in consumer markets, but it's reached the point of diminishing returns. And diversity is not the only chink in standardization's armor. Attempts to build stores in the remaining attractive locations often meet fierce resistance from community activists. From California to Florida to New Jersey, neighborhoods are passing ordinances that dictate the sizes and even architectural styles of new shops. Building more of the same—long the cornerstone of retailer growth—seems to be tapped out as a strategy.

Of course, a company can't customize every element of its business in every location. Strategists have begun to use clustering techniques to simplify and smooth out decision making and to focus their efforts on the relatively small number of variables that usually drive the bulk of consumer purchases.

The customization-by-clusters approach, which began as a strategy for grocery stores in 1995, has since proven effective in drugstores, department stores, mass merchants, big-box retailers, restaurants, apparel companies, and a variety of consumer goods manufacturers. Clustering sorts things into groups, so that the associations are strong between members of the same cluster and weak between members of different clusters.

In fact, by centralizing data-intensive and scale-sensitive functions (such as store design, merchandise assortment, buying, and supply chain management), localization liberates store personnel to do what they do best: Test innovative solutions to local challenges and forge strong bonds with communities.

Ultimately, all companies serving consumers will face the challenge of local customization. We are advancing to a world where the strategies of the most successful businesses will be as diverse as the communities they serve.

W E'RE IN THE EARLY STAGES OF a quiet revolution in consumer markets. For decades, the chains that have dominated the landscape—titans like Wal-Mart, Best Buy, and McDonald's—have pursued single-minded strategies of standardization. They've fine-tuned their store formats, merchandise mixes, and operating and marketing processes, and they've rolled out their winning formulas internationally. They've demanded equally rigorous consistency from suppliers, pushing the standardization ethic deep into consumer product companies and across the entire consumer supply chain.

But the era of standardization is ending. Consumer communities are growing more diverse—in ethnicity, wealth, lifestyle, and values. Many areas, moreover, are now saturated with big-box outlets, and customers are rebelling against cookie-cutter chain stores that threaten the unique characteristics, such as architectural styles and favored brands, of their neighborhoods. When it comes to consumer markets, one size no longer fits all. In response, smart retailers and consumer goods companies are starting to customize their offerings to local markets, rolling out different types of stores, product lines, and alternative approaches to pricing, marketing, staffing, and customer service. They're moving from standardization to localization.

Combining sophisticated data analysis with innovative organizational structures, they're gaining the efficiencies of centralized management without losing the responsiveness of local authority. The greatest benefit of moving from standardization to localization is strategic. Standardized offerings discourage experimentation and are easy for competitors to copy. (Sam Walton openly referred to Kmart as the "laboratory" he copied while growing Wal-Mart.) Customization encourages local experimentation and is difficult for competitors to track, let alone replicate. When well executed, localization strategies can provide a durable competitive edge for retailers and product manufacturers alike.

Reinventing the Big Box

Although standardization has been a powerful strategy in consumer markets, it's reached the point of diminishing returns. Customers are becoming more diverse, according to studies by geodemographers, people who study the population characteristics of specific geographic areas. Measuring ethnicity, age, wealth, urbanization, housing styles, and even family structures, the demographic company Claritas determined in the 1970s that 40 lifestyle segments were sufficient to define the U.S. populace. Today, that number has grown to 66, a 65% increase.

Diversity is not the only nail in standardization's coffin. Many large chains have erected so many stores that they're literally running out of room to expand. They can't open new outlets without cannibalizing old ones. Standardized chains are also meeting with other constraints: Where attractive locations are still available, attempts to build stores often face fierce resistance from community activists. From California to Florida to New Jersey, neighborhoods are passing ordinances that dictate the sizes and even architectural styles of new shops. Building more of the same—long the cornerstone of retailer growth—has been tapped out as a strategy.

Finally, standardization can do the most strategic damage by forcing products and practices into molds. The resulting homogenization of business tends to undermine innovation, all the way up the supply chain. Managers become so focused on meeting tight operational targets—and stamping out exceptions—that they begin to consciously avoid the experimentation that leads to attractive new products, services, and processes. In the end, standardization erodes strategic differentiation and leads inexorably toward commoditization—and the lower growth and profitability that accompany it.

The good news is that there's a way out of standardization's dead end. Technological advances, from checkout scanners and data-mining software to Internet stores and radio frequency identification (a wireless technology that uses small electronic tags to identify and track objects), are providing retailers and their suppliers with deep insight into local preferences and buying behaviors. For the first time, mismatches in supply and demand at individual stores can be pinpointed immediately. The new data make it possible to "localize" stores, products, and services with unprecedented precision. (For an example of the new insights technology can deliver, see the sidebar "Mining the Internet" at the end of this article.)

Our analysis of 30 localization leaders, including Best Buy, Tesco, and VF, documents these benefits. Even Wal-Mart, the sultan of standardization, is moving toward localization. The company has made customization the cornerstone of its "store of the community" strategy, announcing that it plans to tailor formats and products to the local clientele in every store in its chain.

Wal-Mart uses a rigorous process to ensure that customization does not undermine its traditional efficiency. That process begins when a store is still on the drawing board. Company real-estate teams deeply research the local customer base when scouting for locations. Designers then create the store's format by combining suitable templates—stores near office parks, for example, with prominent islands featuring ready-made meals for busy workers. Templates allow Wal-Mart to maintain considerable economies of scale. The company has also developed a sophisticated logistics system, encompassing 110 distribution centers in the United States alone, to manage complex delivery schedules quickly and efficiently.

Through its Retail Link program, Wal-Mart works with suppliers to tailor store merchandise with similar precision. Built on a vast database, Retail Link provides both local Wal-Mart managers and vendors with a two-year history of every item's daily sales in every Wal-Mart store. Using the Retail Link Web portal, Wal-Mart and its suppliers can create maps of local customer demand, indicating which merchandise should be stocked when and where. For example, Wal-Mart stocks about 60 types of canned chili but carries only three nationwide. The rest are allocated according to local tastes. Five years ago, Wal-Mart used just five planograms (diagrams showing how and where products should be placed on retail shelves) to adapt its soup selection to local preferences. Today, with the help of Retail Link, Wal-Mart and its suppliers use more than 200 finely tuned planograms to match soup assortments to each store's demand patterns—raising soup's growth rate by several points in the process. Product companies also use the system to track their sales and inventory levels in Wal-Mart's stores and distribution centers and to develop pricing and marketing programs to boost sales.

Thinking in Clusters

As Wal-Mart and other leaders have discovered, successful localization hinges on getting the balance right. Too much localization can corrupt the brand and lead to ballooning costs. Too much standardization can bring stagnation, dooming a company to dwindling market share and shrinking profit.

Striking the right balance means understanding which elements of a business should be considered for localization, how costly they are to customize, and how much impact they will have from one store to another. Far from being an all-or-nothing game, localization can take place in myriad ways (see the exhibit "What, Where, and When Should We Localize?"). For one retailer, it might make sense to have a highly localized staffing approach but a standardized product mix, while another retailer may warrant the opposite. Similarly, a manufacturer might localize product features in one area and retailer incentives in another. While it may be prohibitively expensive to customize a product to many locations, it may be possible to gain similar benefits by tailoring the product's packaging or promotions at a far lower cost. Wal-Mart found that while ant and roach killer sells well in the southern United States, consumers in the northern states are turned off by the word "roach." After labeling the pesticide as "ant killer" in northern states, the company has seen sales increase dramatically, according to John Westling, senior vice president.

Of course, customization has its limits. Even with rich data, a company can't customize every element of its business in every location. The sheer complexity would be overwhelming, leading to spiraling costs, if not paralysis. That's why leading localizers have begun using clustering techniques to simplify and smooth decision making, focusing their efforts on the relatively small number of variables that usually drive the bulk of consumer purchases.

Rather than letting local managers' decentralized decisions fragment economies of scale, the pioneering companies have developed a science of analyzing data on local buying patterns to identify communities that exhibit similarities in demand. For example, American Eagle Outfitters, a retailer of fashionable casual wear with 740 U.S. stores, found that customers in western Florida exhibited seasonal purchasing patterns and price elasticities that closely matched those of certain

What, Where, and When Should We Localize?

Many different elements of a company's business can be customized, separately or in combination. In consumer markets, a useful way to think about the elements is to arrange them into three categories: what's being sold ("offer"), where it's being sold ("location"), and when it's being sold ("time"). The table provides a generic overview of this organization.

WHAT: Offer Variables

- **Branding**
  - Store (banner names)
  - Product labels
  - Vendor brands
  - Propriety (private brands)
- **Store formats**
  - Size and layout
  - Store design type
- **Merchandise space and assortment**
  - Division
  - Category
  - Department
  - Classification
  - Attributes
    - Style and flavor
    - Color
    - Size
  - Good/better/best range
  - Pack counts
  - Packaging design

- **Pricing**
  - Everyday low vs. high-low policies
  - Ranges
  - Points
  - Matching policies
- **Promotions**
  - Types
  - Temporary price reduction levels
  - In-store displays
  - Markdown policies
  - Frequency
  - Depth

- **Vendor policies**
  - Information sharing
  - Expense sharing
  - Product collaboration
- **Marketing programs**
  - Spending levels
  - Media mix
  - Major messages
- **Store service levels**
  - Store hours
  - Labor quality and schedules
  - Delivery policies
  - Checkout stations
  - Special services (e.g., delivery, repair)

- **Vendor services**
  - Direct store delivery
  - Replenishment and stocking
  - Customer education
- **Operating policies**
  - Inventory levels
  - Sourcing strategies
  - Shrink controls
  - Information sharing

WHERE: Location Variables

Consumer characteristics	**Special Demand Drivers**	**Competitor Characteristics**	**Our Own Store Characteristics**
Demand patterns	School seasons	Store saturation levels	Our market share
Store purchase	Hunting and fishing seasons	Market share	Our store locations
Area purchase	Activities and sights	Store locations	Location characteristics
Geodemographics and	Ski resorts	Store formats	Site quality ratings
attitudes	Beach towns	Pricing levels	Our store formats
Population density	Athletic teams	Promotion policies	Sizes
Age	Tourist attractions	Marketing programs	Design types (models)
Income	Military bases		Condition
Marital status	Special events		Square footage allocation
Ethnicity	Cinco de Mayo		Special fixtures and displays
Religion	Pioneer Day		Merchandise placement zones
Lifestyle segment	Religious holidays		Stores of our sister divisions
Psychographic	Climate zone		Locations
	Temperature		Merchandise mix
	Precipitation		
	Potential weather events		

WHEN: Time Variables

- Hour
- Day
- Week
- Month
- Season
- Year

communities in Texas and California. By tailoring assortments and promotions to such clusters of locations
rather than to individual stores, companies like American Eagle can benefit from customization while holding
on to most of the efficiencies of standardization.

The customization-by-clusters strategy, which Bain
first applied to grocery stores in 1995, has proven effective in drugstores, department stores, mass merchants,
big-box retailers, restaurants, apparel companies, and a
variety of consumer goods manufacturers. Clustering
sorts things into groups, or clusters, so that the associations are strong between members of the same cluster
and weak between members of different clusters. Clusters enable manageable, modular operations—think
again of Wal-Mart's store templates—that capture most
of the benefits of customization while also simplifying
decisions and protecting economies of scale. Consider a
merchandise manager who has to decide how to stock
100,000 items in 1,500 stores for 365 days each year. If
she wanted to customize the mix, she would have to
make about 54.8 billion decisions ($100,000 \times 1,500 \times 365$),
many of which would be based on such small sample
sizes that the predictions of even sophisticated models
would be meaningless. If, however, the merchandise
could be clustered into 2,500 classifications, the stores
could be clustered into 20 similar types (for example,
Latino border locations or upscale suburban places), and
the timing (back to school, winter holidays) could be
broken into 52 weeks, the number of decisions would be
reduced to 2.6 million, which a modern computer model
can optimize fairly easily. (For a discussion of a particularly powerful statistical technique used in sorting
through many variables, see the exhibit "CHAID: Clustering by the Numbers.")

Best Buy is using clustering to move away from a standardized big-box strategy. It has revamped close to 300 of its 700 U.S. stores, introducing "customer-centric" formats to appeal to local shoppers. The company identified five representative types of customers. First, there's "Jill," a busy mother who is the chief buyer for her household and wants quick, personalized help navigating the world of technology. In Eden Prairie, Minnesota, the company designed a store that caters to the needs of this busy suburban moms segment. The company found that this group of previously untapped consumers offered the best opportunity for expansion in the region. To attract this group, the store has an uncluttered layout with wider aisles and warmer lighting, and technology-related toys for children. Personal shopping assistants educate technology neophytes about products, and there's more floor space allocated to household appliances. Although the store still serves other, more traditional electronics shoppers, the company hopes the store can boost its sales by attracting a set of local customers that have felt overwhelmed inside a Best Buy store.

Other stores are being designed around the remaining four types of customers and are based on local demand patterns. For example, there's "Buzz," a technology junkie who wants the latest gear for entertainment and gaming. Stores catering to Buzz have lots of interactive displays that allow shoppers to try out new equipment and media. Then there is "Barry," an affluent, time-pressed professional who is looking for high-end equipment and personalized service. Stores tailored to his needs feature a store-within-a-store for pricey home-theater setups. Stores made with "Ray" in mind emphasize moderately priced merchandise with attractive financing plans and loyalty programs for the family man

CHAID: Clustering by the Numbers

One of many clustering techniques is called CHAID, short for chi-squared automatic interaction detection. A statistical classification method proposed by G.V. Kass in 1980, CHAID sorts items into groups that are statistically different with respect to criterion or outcome. For example, if we want to know what groupings are associated with store profitability, CHAID might show us that money-losing stores are in high-income neighborhoods with multiple competitors, while the most profitable stores are in rural areas and have the capacity to carry the full product assortment.

A significant benefit of CHAID is that it enables us to analyze the effects of characteristics in combination rather than independent from one another. For example, adding playgrounds to Burger King restaurants may have no impact on average but could be very profitable in suburban restaurants near high populations of young children and very unprofitable in downtown locations with expensive real estate and few children.

Let's demonstrate the process with a department store chain we'll call SuperStuff.

CHAID begins with a list of every store in the SuperStuff system and as much information as possible about each—including sales data by location, time, and item. There is no need to worry about entering too much information, since CHAID will highlight only the variables that create statistically significant differences.

We can then use CHAID to find the combinations of characteristics that best explain any variable we choose to explore. In the example "Assessing Store Profitability," we used CHAID to understand what drives EBIT margins (earnings before interest and taxes) among SuperStuff's 508 department stores. CHAID begins, at the top, by showing us that the average EBIT margin is 4.2% for SuperStuff's entire population of stores.

CHAID then identifies the first differentiator of EBIT margins as the presence of at least one KillerMart in each SuperStuff store's trade area. The 198 SuperStuff stores with no nearby KillerMarts have an EBIT margin of 6.4%. The 310 SuperStuff stores near KillerMarts have an average EBIT margin of only 2.8%. Sensible, but not terribly surprising so far. The next steps are where CHAID proves most valuable.

For the 310 stores near a KillerMart, CHAID finds that household income levels drive significant profit differences. The 188 stores in neighborhoods with household incomes of more than $50,000 have average EBIT margins of 3.9%. The remaining 122 stores have margins of only 1.1%.

The data also enables CHAID to generate remodeling ideas. Of the 188 stores in higher-income neighborhoods near Killer-Marts, the 113 that have allocated more than 50% of their square footage to apparel have EBIT margins of 5.3%. The 75 stores with less than 50% allocated to apparel have EBIT margins of only 1.8%. Apparently, plentiful apparel assortments in high-income areas can help SuperStuff to profitably compete against KillerMart's offering.

Jumping to the right-hand side of the CHAID tree, we learn about stores that don't face KillerMarts. In those areas, the 76 large-format stores have an average EBIT margin of 9.1%, almost twice as much as the 122 small or midsize stores, which have a margin of only 4.7%. Furthermore, the 60 small or midsize stores that priced an average market basket of groceries less than 3% above SuperStuff's overall average had an EBIT margin of only 1.2%. However, the 62 small or midsize stores with prices more than 3% above SuperStuff's average have a margin of 8.1%—almost seven times more than the 60 stores pricing less than 3% above the average. It seems that small or midsize stores may do better by raising prices in less competitive markets.

While CHAID certainly doesn't provide all the answers, it can help to surface testable hypotheses such as the following:

· When opening new stores, avoid locations near KillerMarts.

· If there is a KillerMart in the area (or one coming soon), position stores in the highest-income neighborhoods.

· When remodeling stores, especially those near KillerMarts, consider allocating more than 50% of the floor space to apparel.

· Smaller stores in areas without KillerMarts should test price increases.

(continued)

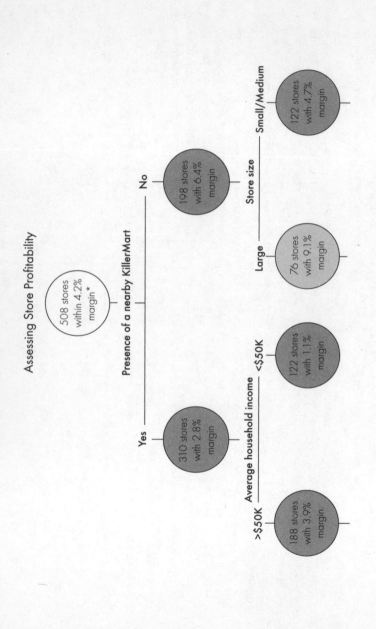

Assessing Store Profitability

508 stores within 4.2% margin*

Presence of a nearby KillerMart

Yes — 310 stores with 2.8% margin

No — 198 stores with 6.4% margin

Average household income

<$50K — 122 stores with 1.1% margin

>$50K — 188 stores with 3.9% margin

Store size

Large — 76 stores with 9.1% margin

Small/Medium — 122 stores with 4.7% margin

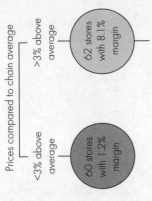

Prices compared to chain average

<3% above average
>3% above average

60 stores with 1.2% margin
62 stores with 8.1% margin

Conclusion:
In areas without KillerMarts nearby, build large stores if possible.

Conclusion:
In areas without KillerMarts nearby, smaller stores should keep prices at least 3% above SuperStuff's average.

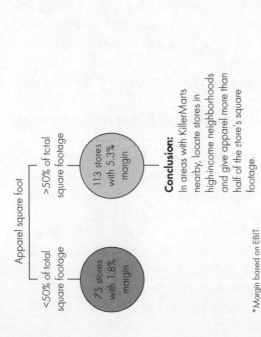

Apparel square foot

<50% of total square footage
>50% of total square footage

75 stores with 1.8% margin
113 stores with 5.3% margin

Conclusion:
In areas with KillerMarts nearby, locate stores in high-income neighborhoods and give apparel more than half of the store's square footage.

* Margin based on EBIT.

on a budget who wants technology that can enhance his home life. Finally, for small-business customers, there's a set of stores with specially trained staffs, extensive displays of office equipment, and mobile "Geek Squads" of service technicians.

While the chain plans to phase out these individual names beneath its banner, the terminology helped Best Buy crystallize the vision of each target customer for each cluster of stores.

By customizing stores in clusters, rather than individually, Best Buy has been able to maintain many of the scale economies that have long underpinned its success. So far, the new strategy is delivering strong results. The 85 Best Buy stores that had been localized as of early 2005 posted sales gains two times the company's average. Encouraged, the company is accelerating the conversion, with plans to change over all its U.S. stores in three years and localize outlets in other countries as well.

So how do you get started with clustering? Begin by collecting as many data as possible on key elements of your business for each store. (Use the exhibit "What, Where, and When Should We Localize?") If some information is missing or hard to get, don't wait for it to be collected. Use what's readily available to launch the analysis, recognizing that clustering always gets better over time. Use the data to develop clusters and identify customization opportunities. Then estimate the economics (including both sales and costs) of localizing the most promising elements of the customer offering—using as few clusters as possible. A clothing retailer, for example, might find that localized markdown policies offer attractive returns and that climate is the key variable influencing markdown decisions. Further analysis may determine that a small number of store clusters—three, say—will be sufficient to gain the optimum economic benefit. For merchandise mix, by contrast, the key variable might be customer lifestyle, which may require a dozen clusters to get the maximum payoff.

Diversity in the Product Line

As big retailers shift away from standardization, the ripple effects will reshape the entire consumer supply chain. Consumer goods companies will need to introduce more variations into their lines, collaborating closely with retailers to put the right products in the right places at the right times with the right pricing and promotion programs. Manufacturers in general have been slow to make this change. Although they conduct extensive consumer research to develop specialized products for unique segments, they have little confidence that rigid retailers will sort, merchandise, and market custom products to the right customer clusters. Products developed for senior citizens will pile up in college communities—slowing inventory turns, forcing costly markdowns, and often leading retailers to drop potentially profitable niche products.

Nevertheless, as growing numbers of retailers are rolling out their own versions of Wal-Mart's Retail Link—including Lowe's (LowesLink) and Target (Partners Online)—a handful of consumer product companies are seizing the advantage by learning to localize. When one food company introduced low-calorie versions of some of its snack foods, it shipped additional cases to stores near Weight Watchers clinics. Cadbury added kiwi-filled chocolate Cadbury Kiwi Royale in New Zealand. Kraft developed Post's Fiesta Fruity Pebbles ready-to-eat cereal especially for Hispanics. Coca-Cola has developed four canned, ready-to-drink coffees for Japan, each formulated for a specific region. Procter & Gamble introduced Curry Pringles in England and, later, Spanish Salsa flavor in England and other parts of Europe and Funky Soy Sauce Pringles in Asia. Frito-Lay developed Nori Seaweed Lay's potato chips for Thailand and A la Turca corn chips with poppy seeds and a dried tomato flavor for Turkey.

One of the leading localizers is consumer products giant VF, a $6 billion apparel maker that owns such popular jeans brands as Lee and Wrangler as well as upscale labels including Nautica and North Face. VF integrates many data sources to identify customization opportunities—to the delight of retailers and consumers. "It is not unusual for localization to improve sales by 40% to 50% while simultaneously reducing store inventories and markdowns," says Boyd Rogers, VF's president for supply chain. "We consider our localization capabilities to be one of our most powerful competitive advantages."

VF combines third-party geodemographic and lifestyle data with daily store-level sales data, extensive consumer research, and competitor analysis to develop localization strategies with retailers, such as Kohl's. VF has found, for instance, that while many buyers now desire lighter-weight denim, male Hispanics still prefer heavier weights. Women in southern California tend to buy shorter denim skirts than those in northern California. Even stores in the same metropolitan area can exhibit very different demand patterns for jeans and other clothes. A store in a community with a large immigrant population, for example, will tend to have greater demand for smaller-size clothing than a store surrounded by nonimmigrant Americans—a subtle testament to America's obesity problem.

For one U.S. chain, VF created 40 clusters, based largely on consumer lifestyle segments and purchasing patterns. Product assortments, marketing strategies, and supply chain systems are tailored to each cluster. VF uses rapid data exchanges to study each store's daily point-of-sales data—not just to replenish shelves but also to discover new demand trends in colors and styles and foster innovation. Through such efforts, VF and its retailers are boosting sales substantially while also avoiding markdowns and returns.

Central Control, Local Touch

A shift to localization raises big management and organizational challenges. The early movers are, in fact, breaking through the old "centralization/decentralization compromise." But it's tricky. Executives' first instinct is often to empower local managers, giving them control over, say, the selection of products on store shelves or major promotional programs.

Such decentralization often backfires, for two simple reasons. First, local managers lack the depth of data, and often the skill, to make consistently smart decisions about buying, merchandising, and operations. Second, giving local managers too much leeway can introduce costly complexity and inconsistency into a business. Indeed, our research found that large manufacturers are less willing to collaborate with, or offer their best terms to, highly decentralized retailers.

J. C. Penney discovered this the hard way in the late 1990s, when it ran into problems by allowing store managers to determine order quantities. Local managers turned out to be too conservative. Seeking to minimize risk, they would buy a wide variety of goods rather than concentrate on hot items. As a result, the stores ran out of popular products quickly and were left with swollen stocks of slow sellers. And because headquarters lacked information on what was in each store, central managers couldn't even see the problems. Between mid-1998 and the end of 2000, Penney's stock price plummeted from $54 to $8.

Then, in 2000, Penney's embarked on a successful turnaround program under the direction of its then-new CEO, Allen Questrom. Penney's went from a decentralized company whose buying and markdown decisions were made at the stores to a centralized, data-driven organization. The management team classified stores into seven clusters on the basis of size and customer demand patterns, developed merchandise and fixture modules, and consolidated purchase orders. It also developed demand-based optimization techniques—allowing product and price ranges, replenishment policies, as well as the timing and depth of markdowns, to be tailored to store clusters. Over the next five years, Penney's stock price more than tripled. Comparable department store sales (sales of stores open for 12 consecutive months), having eroded 2.3% in 2000, rose 3.4% in 2001 and 5% in 2004.

As Penney's discovered, efficient localization requires that most decisions be coordinated centrally, by managers with a broad view of demand patterns and sufficient store-level data to distinguish real insights from random noise. To support headquarters decision makers, leading retailers are building sophisticated information systems that draw from many sources—census and other demographic research; data from store scanners and loyalty cards; consumer surveys and unsolicited comments;

Internet sales data; data from third-party syndicators like AC-Nielsen; and intelligence on competitors. Local managers and personnel are also critical sources of information—often picking up signals that computerized systems can't see. When Wal-Mart, for example, introduced kosher food to its store in Berryville, Arkansas, it was acting on a recommendation from the store manager. The company's other data sources had not uncovered the nearby Jewish community.

Central coordination is also essential to forging close relationships between retailers and product suppliers. Product manufacturers have deep knowledge about how goods sell across all stores in a region. Retailers have equally deep knowledge about how products sell across their networks of stores. Combining those two troves of information allows for a much more comprehensive understanding of both local demand patterns and the way they may cluster across regions.

Leading from the center does not mean that local managers become unthinking robots. In fact, by centralizing data-intensive and scale-sensitive functions such as store design, merchandise assorting, buying, and supply chain management, localization liberates store personnel to do what they do best: Test innovative solutions to local challenges, engage with store guests, and forge strong bonds with their communities. Wal-Mart's store managers are legendary for highlighting hot items and responding to local pricing challenges. Best Buy encourages store employees to create and test hypotheses and share what they have learned throughout the chain. One Best Buy employee recently hypothesized that she could raise store sales by making iPods easier to find. She moved a display to the front of the store, created a shirt

that said, "iPods here," and raised the store's sales rank-
ing from 240th to 69th. 7-Eleven knows that corporate
headquarters could never predict a busload of football
players arriving on a Friday night, but the store manager
can. Combining the efficiencies of a national chain with
the entrepreneurial touches of a mom-and-pop convenience store, 7-Eleven has created a system that it calls
"centrally decentralized."

A World of Difference

Localization isn't free. The shift requires greater investment in data collection and analysis. And however
sophisticated the clustering effort, some economies of
scale will need to be sacrificed—in purchasing, marketing, manufacturing, and store construction. Most companies will want to focus their initial efforts on areas
offering the greatest and quickest return. For example,
the investment is typically lower and the payback faster
on localizing markdowns (typically less than one year)
than localizing base prices (often two years or more). But
as localization skills grow, so do localization opportunities. The systems, data, and organizational processes
that first enable a company's leap to localized markdown
strategies greatly ease subsequent steps to the localization of pricing, promotion, and marketing programs.
(For examples of retailers pushing the frontiers of localization, see the sidebar "Extreme Localization" at the
end of this article.)

Ultimately, all companies serving consumers will face
the challenge of local customization. It's often been
assumed that globalization implies ever-greater homogenization of businesses and their products and services.
The world, in this view, will be packed with indistin-

guishable big boxes selling the same goods and services to everyone. But a look at the emerging localization strategies of the leading companies in consumer markets—companies that once shunned customization but now embrace it—reveals how mistaken this assumption is. We are advancing to a world where the strategies of the most successful businesses will be as diverse as the communities they serve.

Mining the Internet

MANY RETAILERS HAVE OPENED online stores to complement their traditional outlets. But the Web is not just a sales channel; it's also a powerful means of collecting data on variations in local demand. Because online stores can offer extensive ranges of products to national, or even global, customer bases, they can track consumer demand patterns much more broadly and precisely than physical stores can. In a traditional store, after all, you never know what the demand might have been for a product you don't have on the shelves. Online stores use centralized merchandise pools to avoid local stock-outs, and excess demand can often be back-ordered for future delivery. By carefully tracking the home addresses of online buyers as well as the products they're buying (or avoiding), chains that maintain Internet stores can use online sales data to inform decisions about what merchandise to stock in which store. And because the online data can be collected in real time, shifts in physical stores' merchandise mixes can be made quickly to respond to spikes in local demand.

Extreme Localization

WHILE LOCALIZERS TYPICALLY customize 5%–25% of a standardized format, extreme localizers are developing a range of new—but closely related—shopping formats to give targeted customers more convenient purchasing options. This is not conventional segment-based expansion, where retailers build portfolios of brands to serve different sets of customers (think Talbots for women, Talbots for men, and Talbots for kids). Rather, this is sophisticated localization based on insights into three emerging trends in consumer markets:

Trend: Consumer purchasing patterns vary not just by segment but also by purchase occasion. Cross shopping is increasing. The same consumers who buy their computers at a big-box electronics store are heading to a neighborhood electronics shop to pick up one-off peripherals (accessories such as mice, printer cartridges, and cables). By way of response, Best Buy is turning insights from its customer-centric stores into new store formats that draw targeted segments of customers who don't always want to slog through the big box. They are testing out smaller, more convenient stand-alone formats with the launch of Geek Squad stores; Escape, a store that provides 25- to 29-year-old technology buffs a place to hang out; and Studio D, a cozy, neighborhood technology store for the suburban mom who stocks up for the family at Best Buy's large formats but fills her personal technology needs closer to home.

Trend: Technological advances allow for more meaningful sharing of customer knowledge and supply

costs when chain stores are selling the same items through multiple formats. By capitalizing on common information systems, supply chain logistics, and purchasing processes, Tesco has embarked on extreme localization in the grocery sector—and is increasing margins and service levels in the process. Through its loyalty cards, Tesco sees what, where, and when customers buy across the full range of store formats. On the basis of that knowledge, Tesco has built five specialized food formats in the UK: Tesco Superstore, a traditional grocery store for weekly suburban shopping; Tesco Extra, a one-stop hypermarket for large shopping trips; Tesco Metro, a smaller supermarket for customers in high-density urban areas; Tesco Express, a tiny convenience store tailored to quick trips in local neighborhoods; and Tesco.com for Web shoppers. Each of these formats is, of course, clustered and localized to meet specific needs. Metro stores, for example, often provide sandwiches at lunchtime, then create prepared meals for customers to pick up on their way home for dinner.

Trend: Multiformat customers are generating higher profits and deeper behavioral insights. Bain's research shows that multiformat customers—those, for example, that buy from a chain's superstore, catalog, Web site, and neighborhood store—typically spend two to six times as much with a retailer as single-format customers do. Each positive experience builds scale and loyalty, making customers more profitable to the retailer and less likely to be seduced by competitors at vulnerable decision points. Additional sales generate additional insights into consumer behaviors under a wide variety of shopping conditions. They provide greater opportunities to test innovative approaches.

Small-scale retailers used to count on local knowledge and scarce real estate to protect them from the big boys. But those barriers are crumbling as sophisticated chains stretch information technology and creative formats. Extreme localization pioneers are building powerful platforms for innovation. Better yet, they are finding space for new growth in crowded landscapes and improving their economics and customer loyalty in the process.

Originally published in April 2006
Reprint R0604E

About the Contributors

FREDERICK H. ABERNATHY is the Gordon McKay Professor of Mechanical Engineering and the Abbott and James Lawrence Professor of Engineering at Harvard University.

ERIC ANDERSON holds the Hartmarx Research Professorship and is associate professor of marketing at the Kellogg School of Management at Northwestern University.

LEONARD L. BERRY is Distinguished Professor of Marketing and holds the M. B. Zale Chair in Retailing and Marketing Leadership in the Mays Business School at Texas A&M University. He is also professor of humanities in medicine in the College of Medicine at Texas A&M University System Health Science Center.

KRISTINA CANNON-BONVENTRE was an assistant professor of marketing at Northeastern University in Boston.

XAVIER DRÈZE is assistant professor of marketing at the Wharton School at the University of Pennsylvania in Philadelphia.

JOHN T. DUNLOP was a professor of economics, chairman of the economics department from 1961–1966, and dean of the faculty of arts and sciences from 1969–1973 at Harvard University.

MARSHALL L. FISHER is UPS Transportation Professor for the Private Sector, professor of operations and information management, and codirector of Fishman-Davidson Center for Service and Operations Management at the Wharton School at the University of Pennsylvania in Philadelphia.

SCOTT C. FRIEND is the president and CEO of ProfitLogic, a software company in Cambridge, Massachusetts, that develops merchandising optimization systems.

JANICE H. HAMMOND is the Jesse Philips Professor of Manufacturing, senior associate dean, and director of faculty planning at Harvard Business School.

ANNA SHEEN MCCLELLAND was a research associate at the Wharton School. She has written several articles for *Harvard Business Review* including "Supply Chain Management at World Co. Ltd." with Marshall L. Fisher and Ananth Raman.

JOSEPH C. NUNES is a trader, engineer, translator, editor, and writer.

JOHN A. QUELCH is senior associate dean and Lincoln Filene Professor of Business Administration at Harvard Business School.

ANANTH RAMAN is UPS Foundation Professor of Business Logistics at Harvard Business School.

DARRELL K. RIGBY is a director in the Boston office of Bain & Company.

DUNCAN SIMESTER is the NTU Professor of Management Science at MIT's Sloan School of Management.

VIJAY VISHWANATH is a partner at Bain & Company.

PATRICIA H. WALKER is a partner in Accenture's Retail Industry Group, based in Boston.

DAVID WEIL is a professor of economics at Brown University.

Index